EXPERIENCING ISLAM

EXPERIENCING ISLAM

MOHAMMAD ISHAQ KHAN

STERLING PUBLISHERS PRIVATE LIMITED

STERLING PUBLISHERS PRIVATE LIMITED
L-10, Green Park Extension, New Delhi-110016

Experiencing Islam
© 1997, Mohammad Ishaq Khan
ISBN 81 207 1882 8

PRINTED IN INDIA

Published by Sterling Publishers Pvt. Ltd., New Delhi-110016.
Laserset at Vikas Compographics, New Delhi-110029.
Printed at Prolific Incarporated, X-47, O.I.A. Phase-II, N.Delhi-110020.

To my mentor

Hazrat Mohammad Ahsan Shah
as a token of reverence and gratefulness

مردِ خدا بحــــر بود بے کران

مردِ خدا بارد دُر بی سحاب

مردِ خدا عالم اَزحق   بود

مردِ خدا نیست فقیہ از کتاب

"The man of God is a boundless sea
The man of God rains pearls without a cloud
The man of God is made wise by the Truth
The man of God is not learned from book".

(Maulana Jalaluddin Rumi)

PREFACE

This book is the result of my thoughful reading of the *Quran vis-a-vis* the plight of Muslims in the contemporary world situation. Although preliminary thoughts on the opening verses of the Quran were composed during the turbulent years of 1990-91 in the valley of Kashmir, the idea of exploring them developed in the wake of my unexpected return home from Oxford where, as the Leverhulme Senior Fellow at the Centre of Islamic Studies (February-September, 1992) I worked on a project of major international colloboration concerning "An Atlas of Muslims of South Asia."

There is no limit to evolutionary thought processes that one experiences under the guidance of the Quran. However, the kind of consciousness that grows through a lifetime and thoughtful recitation of the Quranic verses is neither purely spiritual nor absolutely intellectual but what may be described as spiritio-historical. The intrinsic capacity of the Quran for moulding consciousness (and, of course, conscience) at the individual and societal level is, therefore, the heart of both spirituality and historicity of the Islamic tradition. And this is what I have attempted to explain while treading the fine line between subjectivity and objectivity assumed to be hallmarks of personal faith and historical method respectively. At no stage does this analysis of spiritual and historical issues of Islam propose an anatagonism between Islam that might appear to be purely spiritual and the mundane world that might be viewed as wholly secular or historical.

Thanks are due to Professor G.R. Malik and Mr. James Forseyth for going through the typescript, though they hold no responsibility for the author's ideas and views expressed in the book. A word of appreciation for Mr. S.K. Ghai for bringing out the book neatly and expeditiously.

   This book is dedicated to one of the noblest souls of
contemporary Kashmir — Hazrat Mohammad Ahsan Shah — as
a token of my reverence and gratefulness.

Magarmal Bagh   **Mohammad Ishaq Khan**
Srinagar - 190001
Kashmir
June 1, 1996

CONTENTS

INTRODUCTION

I had never imagined or ever intended to write a book which might raise the eyebrows of fellow historians, committed to interpret history within a framework in which the role of the religious factor is underplayed in more than several respects in the name of historical objectivity. Over the years my mind has been preoccupied with the variegated forms of response that Islam has evoked at the individual and societal levels through the ages. With my growing awareness of the problems facing the *umma* there is also a latent consciousness of seeing spiritual malaise as the most vital factor behind Muslims' failure to cope with the challenges of immense magnitude within and outside their societies. But the question that defies answer is whether the so-called "liberal" Muslims or the adherents of "Islamic ideology", miscalled "fundamentalists", have ever addressed themselves to such challenges from a standpoint which we call spiritio-historical.

Spiritio-historical consciousness may be described as the evolving, interacting and continuing process of relating the problems of the soul, heart and mind to the faith one professes and the society one lives in. Since faith and society are integral components of a believer's whole existence on this planet, it would be both areligious and ahistorical to assume that religion and history can transcend each other. Being a natural religion (*din al-fitra*), Islam stresses the middle path, and favours the Quranic concept of unity in diversity. The *Quran* would have lost its universal content and relevance had Allah addressed His Message to Muslims alone. The *Quran* at no stage describes Allah as "the God" of Muslims; nor does Allah address Muslims alone. Instead, the Nourisher of the Worlds (*Rabb al-Alamin*) addresses His creatures as believers (*muminin*), disbelievers (*kafirun*), humankind (*annas*) and men of intellect (*ulul al-bab*).

But man's reason *(aql)*, divorced from the radiant structure of the *Quran* embodying grace *(rahma)*, fortitude *(sabr)*, faith *(iman)*, beneficence *(ihsan)*, trust *(tawakkul)*, balm *(shifa)* and inner guidance *(ilm-i-ladunni)*, always tends to produce a consciousness that either creates false hopes or boundaries in human minds. Rationalism, secularism, socialism, nationalism, liberalism and fundamentalism—or in other words, various forms of Western dogmatism—are more than mere forms of man's reason to reason out problems in the realm of his mind *vis-a-vis* society. Although the Western society has not been monolithic in a strict sense, yet in one respect it has shown remarkable unity of purpose in its efforts at Westernising the world in the name of ideologies. The West's worldviews are, therefore, worldviews in a circumscribed sense. In other words, the West's obsession with this world in the wake of the Renaissance and Reformation has set rolling a process in which even those who defy the West for dividing the world between 'sacred' and 'profane' have found themselves interlocked.

That Muslim societies owe a great deal of the malaise afflicting their moral and intellectual conscience to the influence of the West is a proposition worthy of consideration. If, on the one hand, a conscious attempt at integrating Islam and nationalism has long been visible in the political behaviour of the Arab, the Turkish, the Pakistani, the Indian, the Bangladeshi, the Kashmiri Muslims, and so on, on the other, there has been an ever-growing concern for buttressing the "Islamic worldview" or "Islamic ideology" to counter the influence of nationalist and 'alien' ideologies on the Muslim mind. Not infrequently, the Muslims' obsession with this world sweeps them overboard and makes them lose sight of a deeper spiritio-historical truth. Above all, their concern shifts from following the *Quran* and the *Sunna* to maintaining themselves in worldly power or wresting worldly glory or supremacy from the 'enemies'. The task of serving Allah is, therefore, reduced to the lofty ideal of bringing about a revolution. Since I regard the concept of revolution somewhat alien to Islam, and overloaded with the Western ethos, little wonder, then, that the proponents of carrying out a revolution, resort to the imported technology of power and historical violence. There lies the dilemma of Muslim societies in their historical struggle for national and Islamic identity.

The stupendous task facing Muslims therefore is not so much to preserve Islam as it is to discover themselves in relation to their professed faith and history. However, it must be pointed out that in pursuit of their nationalist or "Islamic" objectives, Muslims too often raise the slogan of 'Islam in danger'. This is nothing short of a blasphemy considering the *Quran's* guarantee for the eternal protection of Islam by Allah Himself. True, Allah fulfils His promise of protecting Islam in response to dedication and sacrifice of His servants; but the point that needs to be stressed is that service to Allah, if devoid of prudential caution, is either bound to end in fanaticism or self-destruction. Wasn't the Prophet Muhammad, in the context of the *Quran*, "a perspicuous warner" against "national vanities" or "crowd passions"?

The threat syndrome is, in fact, the unfolding of a historical process called "Islamisation". Unfortunately, neither Muslims themselves nor the Western interpreters of Islam are profoundly conscious of the twin process of Islam and Islamisation. And nothing could be more dangerous than the ideology of looking at Islam from a position in which the human mind is integrally connected to the dialectic of politics. In such a situation, the role of Islam in the evolution of human civilisations is lost sight of; the politically and economically oppressed appear as 'terrorists', or more correctly, the persecuted as persecutors. Being locked into an exclusively and internationally, publicly dramatised confrontation with the Western values of unrestrained freedom and liberalism, the history of Islam no longer unfolds according to its own inner dynamism, but is seen as a retrograde image of medievalism. Who has reinforced such an image of Islam? One may argue convincingly that such an image has been reinforced time and again by the deep-felt legacy of colonialism. But, sad to relate, the dilemma of their situation is that, under the reeling influence of colonialism, the so-called Muslim "Liberals", "Progressives", or for that matter, adherents of "Islamic ideology" as well, do not know, all things considered, whether they are speaking to particular nationalities or *umma* or the public or themselves. Notwithstanding the shortcomings of their secular and ideological approach to Islam, none the less, their only success lies in reinforcing the image of Islam either as Western-oriented or as ideologically politically motivated.

The need to maintain Islamic identity has to be balanced or conjoined with the believers, God-given right to soul-searching. The Islamic values that Muslim "liberals" and ardent supporters of what is termed "Political Islam" have missed are not denied to the one whose lifelong struggle centres round cultivating them. It is our firm belief that humanity will neither become a political version of the *umma* nor the monolithic monster of the Western imagination in the emergence of new ideology, a "New world order". In the context of the *Quran*, humanity is pluralistic; but behind this pluralism is the unifying force, *Rabb al-Alamin*, and the never-ceasing and never-to-be-cowed-down inner urge of a believer to follow His injunctions for the peace of his soul, heart and mind *vis-a-vis* the challenges to which he is always exposed in Rousseau's 'world of ugly want and insolent riches miscalled civilization, the oppression miscalled order, the error miscalled knowledge'. However multifaceted have been the responses of Muslims in geopolitical situations, the sensitive and crucial fact in the contemporary world situation is that they will continue to rise up, in the name of truth and morality, against all forms of historical tyranny or colonialism.

While Islam has intrinsically been a spiritual force, it must be admitted that it has always evoked multiple responses from its adherents throughout history. While at the individual or spiritual level the response is a matter of conscience, at the societal level it has been interspersed with intricated facts of history or worldly life. Since the former kind of response occurred in the turbulent depths of my soul, heart and mind during a period of crisis this explains that I consider myself to be a refugee from histrionics of every kind in relation to Islam. While professional historians have found themselves trapped in their fields of specialisation, my endeavour has been to raise myself above the narrow grooves of academic constraint in order to swim into the oceans of timeless, serene, sublime truth, that is, discovering man in relation to his cosmos and the Creator. I can only hope that my enquiry into the truth, conducted in unison with the soul, heart and mind, might lead to far broader and more probing discussions than those one hears up and down the boulevards of the academic centres of excellence.

1

THE *QURAN*: OPENING VERSES

The first chapter *(sura)* of the *Quran* begins with the Name of
Allah *(Bismillah)*. Being an essential part of the *Quran*, it has
generally been given an independent number in the first chapter.
For the following *suras*, except the ninth, it serves as an
'introduction' or 'headline', and as such is not numbered.
Bismillah al-Rahman al-Rahim means 'In the Name of Allah, Most
Beneficent, Most Compassionate.'

Let us first try to understand Allah since the *Quran* opens
with His Name. Allah is an unimaginable Supreme Being. He is
the Author of the *Quran* whose verses were revealed to the
Prophet Muhammad (May peace of Allah be upon him!) during
the course of about 23 years following his meditations at the cave
of Hira in Mecca. Each verse of the *Quran* has a context and is
related to the situational demands of the temporal world the
Prophet lived in. Does this mean that since the *Quran* is related to
the historical conditions of the Meccan and Medini life of the
Prophet, it has lost its relevance in the contemporary world
situation? Although my aim is not to begin this study of some of
the opening verses of the *Quran* with an element of doubt, none
the less, it is necessary to bear in mind that every kind of
scepticism or doubt that may initially lurk in our minds is bound
to disappear in the course of our contemplative reading of the
Quran. The more we read the *Quran*, contemplate it, and probe
the questions that it raises in our mind and heart, the more will
we be able to find a gradual transmutation in our thoughts and
behaviour. The change may be sudden and spectacular in certain
exceptional cases, but generally spiritual transmutation moves at
a snail's pace. The transmutation particularly relates to the mind
and heart of the reader. While in some cases the *Quran*
particularly appeals to the mind, in others it captivates the heart.

While in the first category, men gifted with intellect and reason
write commentaries on the *Quran*, in the second, men overcome
with the feeling of intense, indescribable love, make their
presence felt in their societies as embodiments of human love and
universal brotherhood characterising the very core of the Quranic
teachings. The *Quran*, of course, is addressed to men of intellect
(u'lul al-bab). But it would be pertinent to ask whether men of
intellect, in their different interpretations of the *Quran*, have
succeeded in presenting a comprehensive conception of the
universe and of man's relation to it which may be appropriately
described as *Tawhidic Weltanschuung*, embodying the very spirit
of the divine revelation. This is not to belittle the intellectual and
scholastic contributions of the classical or modern interpreters of
the *Quran*. However, the point that I want to make is that human
reason, in both the cases, was usually conditioned by the
exigencies of the societies in which the classical or modern
interpreters lived, or by their own reasoned understanding of the
Quran. Little wonder, therefore, that every interpretation of the
Quran conveys the message of Allah somewhat partially.
Notwithstanding the abiding value of such commentaries of the
Quran ranging from Ibn Kathir to Maulana Ab'ul ala Maududi or
Maulana Abul Kalam Azad, it remains a fact that each interpreter
of the *Quran* is known for the marked trait of his intellect. Ibn
Kathir, for instance, presents the so-called traditional view of the
Quran; and, of course, his commentary has remained the basis of
a plethora of commentaries on the *Quran* produced from time to
time. While Maududi brings home to his readers the religio-
political content of the *Quran* with the unrivalled skill of a
modern *mujtahid*, Abul Kalam Azad, essentially a political
activist, interprets the *Quran* with a view to lending an
intellectual support to the nationalist struggle of the Indian
National Congress against the British imperialism and the two-
nation theory of the Muslim League. However, Azad's
contribution to promoting our understanding of the Quranic
humanism and universalism cannot be denied.[1]

Is it possible that the interpretations of Azad and Maududi
limited their understanding of the *Quran*. And it is for their
motivated interpretations of the *Quran* that a majority of literate
Muslims in South Asia prefer to read what they call traditional,
or, what may be described as undiluted interpretations of the

Quran available in the form of various traditional commentaries based on Ibn Kathir and others.

It is also important to remember that for a vast multitude of illiterate Muslim folk in the subcontinent it is not the traditional or modern scholarly interpretations of the *Quran*, but the Sufic view of the *Quran* that has moulded their sensibilities, sensitivities and social behaviour. Although the Sufis did not write systematic commentaries on the *Quran*, yet in their terse sayings or mystical compositions they explained in beautiful terms the universality of the Quranic message. It is for this reason that the Sufis appealed to both the average intelligence and feeling or touch of the commoners. My purpose in recognising the intrinsic merit of the Sufic understanding of the *Quran* is not to single out their contribution as the only true interpretation of the divine message, nor is it to dramatise the polarity between the so-called 'orthodox' tradition represented by the Ulama and the so-called 'liberal' one represented by the Sufis in the Orientalist fashion; in reality, however, it is to seek an understanding of the *Quran* through both reason and love.

It must be borne in mind that reason and love are a *sine qua non* for promoting a better understanding of the *Quran*. But both reason and love in the context of the divine revelations do not have commonplace meaning as given in the dictionaries. I think that both terms are not mere words but more than concepts so intertwined as to form a single dictionary of the thought of the *Quran*. In the ordinary usage of the word reason, Satan's refusal to bow before Adam may be justifiable since he had been taught to obey only the Creator and not the created. But Satan's rationality turned into disbelief and arrogance when it led him to question the very reason of the Reason. Satan's defiance of the Reason, i.e., Allah, arose not out of his love for the Supreme Reality but out of arrogance bred by his reason. The main reason put forward by Satan to justify his defiance was that while Adam was made of clay he was made of fire; and, therefore, it did not behove a creature, endowed with the characteristic of power, i.e., fire, to prostrate himself before what he thought to be an ordinary creature made of despicable matter. Since among all the angels, Satan was the only creature to argue in such a manner, he earned the Divine wrath not merely for disobedience, but more importantly, for banishing love from his thought or reason. And love in the usage of the *Quran* is not love in the ordinary sense, but surrender to the will of the Supreme Reason. Man is thus essentially a servant of Allah *('abd)* required to think and act in his everyday social behaviour in congruity with the spirit of the *Quran*. Are we then prepared to contemplate the *Quran*? Allah urges us to think on the deeper meaning of the *Quran* rather than merely on its exoteric aspect. The fact is that a deep understanding of the *Quran* demands what may be described as consciousness of a special category *(sha'ur)*. For this reason and also for gaining true knowledge *(ma'rifa)* of Allah, we need to reason out the unreasonableness within our ownselves.

So let us make a sincere attempt to discover the Author of the *Quran* with the supreme consciousness of being His humble servants *('ibad)*.

There is no corresponding word for Allah in the English language. By no stretch of the imagination can the seemingly corresponding word, God, be regarded as a synonym for Allah. The Christian concept of God is fundamentally opposed to the concept of Allah for the union of three persons, Father, Son, and the Holy Ghost, in the one Godhead or, in other words, the threefold personality of the one Divine Being circumscribes the vision of the one God. Unlike the deities of the Hindus, Allah is neither feminine nor plural. When God is described in terms of they or she, He is in danger of losing omnipotence, omnipresence and above all universality. Little wonder that the Hindu concept of God is so fragmented. The Hindus have gods and goddesses, and they are worshipped in various regions as Ram, Hari, Vishnu, Krishna, Kali, Ganesh, Siva and so on.

Contrary to the Christian view of God, Allah does not belong to one particular religion or community or, more correctly, one prophet, but he belongs to the universe. Nor does the pervading concept of the universality of Allah permit the worship of any of the diverse representations of divinity that are to be found in the regions of the world. Moreover, the second verse of the *Quran* *(Alhamud)* enjoins believers in Allah to thank Him. "Praise be to Allah, the (Sole) Nourisher of the Worlds", so goes the second verse.

Bismillah and *Alhamud* are complimentary. When a believer recites the *Quran*, when he is at the dining table, when he starts work at his business establishment or office—in fact, in all his ritual and social actions—he begins with the Name of Allah, Most Beneficent and Most Merciful. And when he performs any ritual or social obligation he praises Allah, the Cherisher and Sustainer of the Worlds. Allah is thus known to us in the first two verses as Rahman, Rahim and Rabb. These are merely attributes of Allah, no more and no less. In the third verse repeated emphasis is on the unbounded graciousness and mercifulness of Allah. It is the Lord of the universe who alone by virtue of His being the Most Beneficent *(Rahman)* and the Most Compassionate *(Rahim)*, deserves to be the Master of the Day of Judgment (verse: iv). While Allah is to be feared and obeyed, at the same time, He has to be loved in view of being Beneficent, Compassionate and Nourisher *(Rabb)*. And a true love for such a Master can be inculcated only when we begin to realise the meaning of the fifth verse that He alone deserves to be worshipped and that He alone is the Universal Power for seeking aid in our spiritual and social endeavours.

On realising in the depths of our souls Allah's love and care, His grace and mercy, and His power and justice (as the Master of the Day of Judgment), the immediate consequence is that we become conscious of our limitations and weaknesses as humans in contrast to His all-embracing and sufficient power. It is here that the necessity for bowing in the act of worship arises. Through such an act 'we' feel that we are associated with all those who seek Allah. Thus our act of worshipping Allah is not merely a ritual in the ordinary sense of the word, but it is a duty generating a unique kind of both spiritual and social awareness in ourselves. This sense of duty towards Allah disciplines our thoughts and actions and creates a strong sense of a fellowship of faith in our consciousness. It is in this sense that believers in Allah form a single community *(umma)*.

The next verse of the opening chapter is our prayer in seeking Allah's succour in guiding us to the Right Path. Here the question arises: which is the Right Path? The answer lies in the subsequent verse, i.e., the last verse of the first *sura*. Herein Allah shows us the way of those on whom He bestowed His grace. With a modicum of spiritual insight it would not be difficult for us to see the people who walked in the light of His grace. From the viewpoint of the *Quran*, such people are His messengers, and prophets, right from Adam to the Prophet Muhammad (May

peace of Allah be upon him), who were vouchsafed His grace
since they did not wander aimlessly in the world but in their
desire for seeking Allah's guidance found the straight way. The
way of Allah is the way of grace, of peace, of harmony. And
people who followed the way of Allah under the spiritual
leadership of their prophets earned for them various titles in the
Quran, such as, the pious *(muttaqin)*, upright *(salihun)*, believers
(muminun), believing women *(muminat)*, those near to Allah
(muqarrabun), and so on. But people who strayed from the
Straight Path earned the wrath of Allah. Hence the first chapter of
the *Quran* ends not only with the prayer asking Allah for His
grace but also for His protection against His wrath in the
eventuality of our straying from the Path because of our actions.

In either case, then, our actions are responsible for His grace
or wrath. The grace of Allah stands not only for the peace of our
innermost selves, but it, also, can contribute a great deal towards
real peace in the world order by way of our actions deriving
sustenance from His grace. Contrary to Allah's grace, His wrath
can disturb not only our mental equilibrium but also the world
order. Thus a person who does not seek Allah is spiritually
doomed. He may be successful in worldly life; he may have
attained to the heights of worldly glory. But, alas! his worldly
glory ends with him or, in certain cases, before his own eyes. On
the other hand, the man who seeks Allah and lives in the world as
a traveller in His path is sure to reach the acme of his spiritual
desires and even spiritual excellence.

There is a mighty chasm indeed between the man who seeks
the world and the man who seeks Allah. While the one runs after
the world, the other finds the world running after him. In the first
category, men do contribute to the growth and development of
the worldly order by way of their enterprising skill, scientific
researches, and above all, intellect. Notwithstanding worldly
men and women's achievements in the field of medical science
and technology, the positive gains of their efforts have been
somewhat neutralised by the state power that arrogates to itself
the prerogative of determining the future of the world by virtue
of being in possession of superior technology. In other words,
then, the human efforts of scientists which could have been better
utilised for removing hunger, disease and ignorance in the world
are used against one nation or the other in the name of

maintaining the balance of power in the world. The scale of destruction and devastation caused by the two World Wars has not deterred men from producing sophisticated weapons, not for the good of the world's inhabitants but rather for their destruction. The role of the United States, in which state power is effectively wielded by what President Eisenhower called the "military industrial complex" provides the best example of how an apparently great world power derives its authority from the superior strength of its technology rather than from God. The United States has set itself the task of playing a dominant role in the contemporary global situation in accordance with its interests. Wasn't Washington's decisive intervention after the Iraqi invasion of Kuwait actuated by its economic interests? While no sensible person can afford to be sympathetic to Saddam Hussain for his self-inflicted troubles, at the same time, one should not think in terms of assigning a liberator's role to George Bush. If such were the case, the US and its allies world have since genuinely intervened to stop the genocide of masses of humanity in Bosnia or elsewhere in the world. The US supported the Afghan Mujahideen so long as its interest in weakening the USSR was served at the altar of a people drawn into a bloody struggle by the opposing ideologies of the so-called superpowers. Did the so-called liberating ideologies of the two superpowers leave any seminal impact on the people of Afghanistan?

The fact is that the 'super' powers' role in the Muslim world has only served to strengthen the fears and suspicions of Muslims against them. Historically, both the West and the communists have always been severe in their criticism of "fundamentalism" *vis-a-vis* their liberating ideologies. But in their diatribes against 'fundamentalism', those powers have seldom realised that it is not simply their denunciation but, also, their own ill-fated policies that have served the cause of what they call 'Islamic fundamentalism'. While I find no reason, strictly from the viewpoint of the *Quran,* to lend any intellectual support to 'liberal' forces of the West and their allies or adherents in the contemporary Muslim majority or minority situations, it must also be borne in mind that Western perceptions of fundamentalism are overloaded with ingrained American notions. *The Random House Dictionary of the English Language* defines fundamentalism as "a movement in the American

Protestantism that arose in the early part of the 20th century and
that stresses the infallibility of the *Bible* in all matters of faith and
doctrine, accepting it as a literal historical record". Viewed
against such twentieth century origins and connotations of
fundamentalism, the Western view of Islamic resurgence
movements is stereotypical and presumptuous. However, what
gives a superficially authentic appearance to "Islamic
fundamentalism" is not so much the individual urge of centuries
past to revive the pristine values of the primordial *din* in
accordance with the *Quran* and the *Sunna* as it is an orchestrated
social response to fight the onslaught of Western forces against
Islam on religio-political grounds. The so-called "Islamic
fundamentalism" is not fundamentalism as such; in actual reality,
it is the vehicle of protest, using Islam as an ideology of religio-
political mobilisation, against the ethnocentrism of the West. Not
the least, replication to Islam in a perceived euphoric sense of its
past political glory, seems to me a defence mechanism devised to
combat all that is contrary to purely historical expression or
assertion or restatement of *ummatic* identity.

Although imperialism is supposed to be dead, it lives on; not
least in the form of an attitude of cultural superiority that has
become the cherished legacy of the West. That the West continues
to regard the liberal values as central to what is actually worldly
ideology is amply borne out by its disregard for the religious
susceptibilities of Muslims. Thus the underlying spirit that
informs 'liberal' ideology of the West not only paints Islam in
lurid colours through sustained electronic propaganda, but also
projects psychopathic personalities among Muslims as crusaders
for Western values (for example, Salman Rushdie and Taslima
Nasreen).

One may earnestly ask whether the West's arrogance in
respect of Islam and Muslim peoples can possibly have any
meaningful relationship between the West and the so-called
Muslim world.

It follows that the world of today is far more divided than it
was before. Can a better understanding of the *Quran* help us
promote the cause of stability and harmony in the contemporary
global situation? Can we build bridges of understanding on the
basis of its eternal message? I particularly refer to the *Quran*
because in the years to come believers in Allah and His Book are

destined to play a crucial role in shaping the course of world history. In which direction is the world order moving? This pertinent question has repeatedly been asked; and it figured particularly when there only existed two ideologies in the world, namely, Communism and Capitalism. But the collapse of Communism in its own haven in recent times has shown that ideologies belong to the realm of particularities. It is ahistorical to explain the failure of Communism in terms of a single factor; in fact, future historians would be in a better position to explain the multiplicity of factors that brought about the collapse of Soviet communism in a little over seven decades. In terms of history, seven decades do not provide any justification for Communists to claim their ideology as having universal validity. In the Communist system, man was reduced to a machine. His identity as the pride of creation was eroded. His sole object in a given social order was the pursuit of material development. But even in doing so he could not improve his lot relatively in contrast to the Western man who enjoyed freedom. Communism has died because it rested on force. It did not take into consideration human urges and volitions. What, however, gave a segment of stability to the Communist regimes over the last seven decades was the common urge of people to fight the exploiter in order to establish a classless society. It was in the name of such a Utopian ideology that the world stood divided between two power blocs for over half a century. Communism was a threat to Capitalism, so was the latter ideology to the former. But how is it that Capitalism seemingly overcame Communism? Is the exploiter destined to spread his tentacles in history?

One of the greatest contributions of Karl Marx to human history was that he was able to identify the devil in society, i.e., the exploiter. Marx was against all forms of exploitation. Although his social philosophy was mainly based on his understanding of the history of Western Europe, yet it had universal relevance in terms of its appeal to the common man groaning under the weight of social, economic, political and even religious exploitation in the East. It was for this reason that the Communist revolution shook the industrially backward regions of the East. It is a marvel of history that the revolution which Marx and Engels expected to take place in an industrially developed society, however, took place in an agriculturally backward country like Russia. The very fact that Marxists did not see the triumph of their ideology in the industrially developed countries of the West points to some inherent weakness in Marx's Utopian scheme.

The failure of Marxism in the West may be explained mainly in terms of the Westerner's receptivity to reason. The Renaissance and Reformation movements that took place in medieval western Europe were solely guided by reason. These movements left a deep imprint not only on the minds of the West, but in turn, led to the development of human personality to such great heights that thenceforth its sole aim came to be the universe.

The Westerner did not turn a deaf ear to Marx. Instead he devised ways to combat an ideology which, though based on the nobler intentions of eradicating social inequalities, was bound to create an inequality of the worse type in the world order. It was an inequality of an unimaginable kind. In Marx's grandiose scheme of the world order, man was conceived to be subject to the governing forces of production. His thought and behaviour were entombed in an inanimate productive technology. No wonder, for over half a century, people in the USSR acquiesced in the supremacy of the economic law of production over their mental make-up. In defence of ideology, man in the USSR, although gifted with intellect, wisdom and love, sought to sever all connections with his Creator. He sought to destroy the very foundations of faith in the Almighty on the basis of his reason, determined by the economic law of motion. The historians sought to give intellectual support to the Communist ideology by way of overemphasizing the supreme importance of the economic factor over all others. Human history, though full of complexities and even mysteries, was so easily defined that scores of histories lending both credence and sustenance to the ideology were manufactured in conformity with the economic model. History became dogma in the hands of Soviet historians. But when history is reduced to a dogma, it itself creates conditions against the narrow confines within which it is sought to be explained or, for that matter, even perpetuated in man's consciousness.

The unfolding of the recent historical drama in the Soviet Union therefore needs to be understood against the background of man's historical error in making his faculties and also future subservient to inanimate forces of production or, in other words, technology. History, if studied in totality, will bring us close to the consciousness that we aim to achieve through reflecting on the book of the Master of the universe—the Eternal Owner of all productive forces in the world. Among innumerable productive forces, the *Quran* assigns primary importance to two, i.e., love and reason. Although we seek to study the opening verses of the second chapter of the *Quran* through love and reason, at the same time, our attempt would be to arrive at an understanding of the *Quran* in the total context of several other complex forces which contribute to the making of human history.

Without probing the first verse of the second chapter *alif, lam, mim* in view of its deep mystical meaning or subjecting its alphabets by way of rational analysis to something other than Allah means them to be, we would reflect on the second verse which is directly addressed to man. It is categorically stated that the *Quran* is, without an iota of doubt, the Book of Guidance for the pious *(hudan lil muttaqin).*[2]

The second verse of the first chapter and that of the second *sura* are not only complementary but eye-openers for us. While in the one Allah urges us to praise Him as the Master of the Worlds, in the other He undoubtedly describes His book as guidance for the pious. Allah, as the universal guide *(Hadi)* begins His discourse on universalism rather than on particularism. Here the *Quran* appeals to human reason. Allah proclaims for Himself not only undisputed Lordship but simultaneously and repeatedly regards the internal piety of believers as a norm of universal applicability.

Believers in Allah are thus united in His cause which stands for the universal rather than a particular good of human kind. The *Quran* was revealed for this purpose alone rather than for confining its universal message to a particular group of believers proud of calling themselves Muslims or adherents of Islam. The purpose of revelation was, also, to open the doors of an inter-religious dialogue in a spirit of tolerance, faith and sensitivity.

O people of the Book: Let us come together upon a formula which is common between us—that we shall not serve anyone but Allah, that we shall ascribe no partner to Him, and that none of us shall take others for lords beside Allah. And if they turn away, then say: Bear witness that we are they who have surrendered (unto Him).[3]

Unfortunately, those who surrendered unto Allah (Muslims) have, in certain cases, reduced the *Quran* to a ritual or a dogma or ideology rooted in the temporal situation. The aim of the *Quran* has never been to establish a universal Islamic state; rather, it has been to ensure the universality of *din*, as defined in the *Quran*, in the pluralistic structure of His own created world order:

> And if your Lord had willed, He would have made mankind one nation, but they continue to remain divided.[4]

> O mankind! Lo! we have created you male and female, and have made you nations and tribes that ye may know one another. Lo! the noblest of you, in the sight of Allah, is the best in conduct. Lo! Allah is the knower, Aware."[5]

It follows that the purpose of the *Quran* is to make believers in Allah supreme embodiments of universal peace and harmony.

> O mankind! There has come unto you an exhortation from your Lord, a balm for that which is in the breast, guidance and a mercy for believers. Say: In the bounty of Allah and in His mercy: therein let them rejoice. It is better than what they hoard.[6]

The prerequisite for restoring peace in the world order is not the possession of nuclear weapons by state powers so as to ensure a balance of terror in strategically sensitive regions of the world like West Asia and South Asia; rather it is a sincere belief in Allah's grace and mercy that alone can work miracles. We have already somewhat equated His grace with peace, harmony and love *vis-a-vis* His wrath which creates violence, disharmony and hatred consequent upon our own actions.

The contemporary world is a strife-torn world. There is violence everywhere; be it the *intifada* of oppressed Palestinians, the genocide of Muslims in Bosnia-Herzegovina or elsewhere. The Afghans were drawn into a bloody war for over a decade in defence of Islam versus Communism; and in spite of the fact that the Afghan *mujahideen* have formed their own government, the blood of innocent Muslims by Muslims themselves continues to be shed despite the apparent triumph of 'faith' *(iman)* over 'infidelity' *(kufr)*. Even Kashmiri Muslims, known for centuries for non-violence, came to believe that the only way to attain political freedom *(azadi)* was an armed struggle against the Indian armed forces.

While the so-called Third World countries continue to groan under the weight of the legacies of the colonial era, Western powers under the leadership of the United States are seemingly determined to build up a new world order. What will be the ideological basis of the new order that Washington, along with its vanquished rival, is striving to found? Time will show the sincerity behind such human efforts. There is, however, a latent feeling in certain quarters that Washington, which hitherto used Muslim sentiment against the atheism of Marx to her maximum advantage, will not allow the so-called 'Muslim World' to emerge as an effective counterpoise against her ideology deriving sustenance from the dominant concepts, viz., capitalism, secularism, and above all, liberalism. Is the *Quran* opposed to the ideology of the West? Although an answer to this question demands a detailed discussion, it will suffice here to say that the United States ideology stands deeply rooted in the ethos of the history of Western Europe. And, from our standpoint, the very ethos of the Western culture is based on a deeper schism between reason and faith.

'A little knowledge is a dangerous thing', so goes the saying, but I may add that too much of knowledge, based on the so-called supremacy of reason, is more dangerous. Such knowledge does not contribute to the growth of knowledge; rather it breeds ignorance, friction, rivalry and discord. Knowledge, based on mere supremacy of reason, is sheer ignorance and arrogance. Such knowledge, even if rooted in a human urge to fight social inequalities, is liable to breed hatred, suspicion and pride. The divide between the people of the West and those of the former Soviet Union was actually based on compartmentalisation of knowledge as a sequel to the intellectual efforts at overemphasizing the significance of one factor over the other. To cap it all, the ideologues of the West sought to define knowledge of society within the confines of their partial reason or discursive reason; hence ideology became a dogma, no less no more.

It follows that the Western man is determined to be guided in the future course of the development of his society by reason alone rather than by faith. His obsession with the supremacy of reason has led him time and again to question the very basis of faith. This is not to suggest that there are no faithful Christians in the West. For, indeed, there is no dearth of such people in the

West. But it remains a fact that even the faithful among Westerners are so preoccupied with the triumphant march of reason that they take great pride in labelling themselves more as creatures of logic than faith. Thus, for instance, the Christian missionaries struggled for centuries to show that while Christianity stood for peace based on the rationality of its ethical values, Islam, on the other, bred violence, hatred and superstition. The whole mass of Orientalist literature, with certain honourable exceptions, was produced with the sole object of distorting the image of Islam. One baneful effect of such intellectual endeavours was that the image of Muslims in the consciousness of Western man came to be that of volatile, arrogant and superstitious people. While the Christian missionaries left no stone unturned in presenting Islam and Muslims as irrational categories, the *Ulama* did not lag behind the church-oriented historians of Islam in Western Europe in presenting their religion as somewhat of a jigsaw puzzle. There is no ordained priesthood in Islam; yet the *Ulama* arrogated to themselves the exclusive prerogative of being the sole guardians of the Islamic law *(Shari'a)* not solely by dint of their knowledge but, also, on account of their pedigree. Priesthood became so dangerously and irreligiously institutionalised in Muslim societies that the *Ulama* came to be regarded as the standard-bearers of the so-called 'Islamic Orthodoxy', or in other words, the *Shari'a*.

It must be pointed out that four great Sunni teachers—Imam Malik, Imam Ahmad bin Hanbal, Imam Abu Hanifa and Imam Sha'afi—undoubtedly rendered meritorious services to Islam by codifying the religious law *(Shari'a)*. Given the conditions that existed in the Muslim world at the emergence of their four schools of thought, there was indeed no alternative for Muslims other than to adhere to any one of these, keeping in view the ethos of the geographical and cultural environment in which they lived. For several centuries, the system of adherence to a particular school has worked so well that Islam has achieved a greater degree of respectability, stability and popularity than it had achieved during the period when conflicts and controversies raged around Muslim societies about varied questions of religious and social significance. The four great teachers of Islam undoubtedly saved Islam and its adherents from splitting into sects and groups. What added further to the strength of Islam and the unrivalled stature of the four great *imams* was the fact that the Sufis of the main orders owed strict adherence to one of the four schools. A vast bulk of religious literature concerning mainly jurisprudence *(fiqh)* produced during the course of several centuries was the direct outcome of the abiding contribution of the four teachers to Islam.

It is a truism to remark that the four great teachers of Islam closed the door of individual reasoning *(ijtihad)* by codifying Islamic law *(Shari'a)* on the basis of their masterly understanding of the *Quran*, the *Hadith* and the *Sunna*. Although the motive behind such an assertion is historical necessity rather than any religious warrant, it would not be out of place to ask, in our effort at understanding rather than interpreting the *Quran*, whether the Holy Book discourages an individual from forming an opinion on any issue ranging from the yearnings of his soul to that of his worldly needs. The *Quran* intrinsically has a high creative potential to develop in an individual his own reason in consonance with its essential spirit of *Tawhid*. The Prophet Muhammad's reason, in other words, his sayings *(hadith)* and social behaviour *(Sunna)*, developed during the course of about 23 years. The *Quran* was revealed to the man who was essentially gifted with limitless wisdom *(hikma)*. Every verse of the *Quran* revealed to the Prophet was not without a context related to the ethos of the Arab society that he transformed during his lifetime. But one distinguishing characteristic of the Prophet's wisdom was that it was anchored in the ocean of universal love, tolerance and humility. Thus in the *Quran*, while the Prophet Muhammad is called by Allah by various epithets, he is also described as a 'Grace for the Worlds'. Since the Prophet was the human manifestation of Allah's grace, strict adherence to his *Sunna* is traditionally described as obedience to Allah. The Prophet was a perfect example of love, tolerance, mercy and wisdom. A believer is supposed to follow in the footsteps of the Prophet because through his *Sunna* alone can he understand the deep spiritual truths for purposeful and peaceful living contained in the *Quran* and the Prophetic wisdom.

It should not, however, be supposed that adherence to the *Sunna* means blind adherence. We must make a clear distinction between adherence as understood in its dictionary sense and adherence as construed within the framework of the *Quran* and the *Sunna*. In sociological terms, man as a social being, owes allegiance to one group or another in one form or another in the society to which he belongs. No individual can live or work in a world of his own making. He may be apolitical, a recluse and so on; yet he has to adhere himself to a certain model. A religious recluse is commonly understood as free from all fetters, yet undergoes a severe training in the form of penances and abstinence by his strict adherence to a model. And the model before a recluse is his own *guru* or a teacher in the mystic discipline. Similarly, a good government also adheres to a model for serving the interest of the people efficiently in all branches of administration. Governments doing otherwise are the worst examples of corruption, anarchy, misrule and inefficiency.

Adherence to certain norms is thus a natural necessity for healthy development of both individuals and societies. It was this natural law of necessity that required the children of Adam, from the very beginning of the world, to follow a norm or a model. From the viewpoint of the *Quran*, all prophets were sent to teach people to adhere to norms or, in other words, the *Shari'a* of Allah, so that in following the way of His grace the forces of harmony would replace those of discord. The *Quran* is quite explicit on this point. "And verily we have raised in every nation a messenger."[7] But the theme that repeatedly occurs in the *Quran* is that concerning the terrible fate of nations which threw to the winds the admonitions of their prophets and messengers. Although the *Quran* is very critical of the Jews and Christians for distorting the teachings of Moses and Christ, yet it does not reject outright Christianity and Judaism. Thus evidence which testifies to Allah's praise for true believers among 'Christians' is not lacking in the *Quran*.

It would be clear, then, that the necessity for revealing the *Quran* to the last of His Prophets was also born out of an interplay of various historical forces. Allah's purpose was not to create a new religion. But as a result of human actions in defiance of norms enshrined in the revealed books before the *Quran* an inevitable necessity had arisen for renewing the dying traditions of the pristine *din* of Abraham. The Prophet Muhammad did not found a new religion but in the Quranic sense his lifelong struggle saw the successful fruition of the mission of the prophets in the line of Abraham. The Prophet Muhammad's greatest achievement lay in making the volatile and unruly Arabs submit to the Will of Allah in accordance with the Quranic injunctions and his wisdom. It was in this sense that the Abrahamic religion took the form of Islam or complete surrender in the *Quran*. And the people who surrendered to Allah and affirmed their faith in the prophethood of Muhammad thus came to be known as Muslims. The new community of believers also came to be known as *ummat-i-Muhammadiyya* in respect of its unswerving faith in the oneness of Allah, the *Quran* and the finality of the Prophethood of Muhammad.

The fundamental tenet of Islam is *Shahada*, i.e., 'verily there is no God, but Allah who is the one and verily Muhammad is His servant and messenger!' *Kalima-i-Shahada* is not a part of the *Quran*, but the human testament of the Oneness of Allah by Muhammad, the perfect man, through service and mission in that cause. The *Quran* intrinsically addresses Muhammad as Allah's servant *(abd)*, though it brings home to believers in no unamibiguous terms how Allah elevated His servant (a human being) to the pinnacle of spiritual and worldly glory by dint of his response to His revelations. The adherence to the Quranic injunctions and the *Sunna* are the quintessence of Islam since the very foundation of *din* rests on the reciprocity of actions between the Creator and the created. The prophethood of Muhammad (Peace of Allah be upon him) was not a bed of roses; it was full of worldly and spiritual experiences. The worldly experience for Muhammad and his followers was that of innumerable human hardships and sufferings. Muhammad was a perfect model of tolerance in the face of intolerance. He was the very model of serenity, humility, piety, and friendliness in the face of crisis.[8] Such virtues exalted him in the estimation of the *Quran*, and, but for them, he would not have been remembered by Muslims worldwide as the perfect man *(insan-i-kamil)*.[9]

Some human beings have always desired to achieve perfection in pursuit of their goals. An artist aims at perfection through his adherence to a model. The idea of perfection has been at the very root of human activity. Be it music, painting, sculpture, architecture, calligraphy and so on, the spirit behind human endeavours has always been to achieve perfection. Artistic skills produce models of excellence, though not of perfection in the strictest sense. But what is remarkable about artistic production is that it has always been characterised by a spirit of creativity.

The relation of man to Allah is both a matter of creation and perfection in the context of the *Quran*. Allah perfected *din* through a chain of prophets culminating in the human efforts of the last of them, Muhammad, the Seal of prophets. *Din* achieved its perfect glory in all respects during the time of the Prophet Muhammad. Thus Muhammad's *Sunna* became a model for succeeding generations of believers. Muhammad became the ideal of a perfect man for those who voluntarily surrendered to Allah out of conviction or were assimilated in Islam through centuries of an acculturation process.

The Quran had basically sought to unite the warring Arab tribes under the banner of *Tawhidic Weltanschuung*. It was Muhammad who upheld this banner under very trying conditions. For several years in the aftermath of his experience at Hira, Muhammad and his followers were put to a great deal of trouble by the people of Mecca. His arch enemies were both those who were closely related to him and those who had intimately known him from the days of his youth. Abu Jahal and Abu Lahab left no stone unturned in subjecting him to every kind of humiliation and suffering. The magnitude of the sufferings of the Prophet at the hands of his own kith and kin was so immense that in the Holy Book, Allah curses Abu Lahab[10] for his inhuman and shameful act of heaping contumely on him. Viewed rationally, a critic of the *Quran* may express surprise at the act of the Most Compassionate and the Most Merciful Allah cursing an ordinary human being in His revelations. But, as has been pointed out earlier, the key to understanding the deep meaning of the Quranic verses is not our limited reason alone but reasoned love which gradually permeates our consciousness on our regular and thoughtful recitation of the *Quran*. Muhammad is not merely the servant of Allah but he is also the beloved of the Most Merciful. The *Quran* is thus not just an act of Allah performed miraculously in a moment, but it is the culmination of a historical process beginning from the descent of Adam and human responses to His revelations sent through Prophets and messengers. In that sense, the *Quran* is not only divine but also humane since it seeks to establish a unique kind of abiding relationship between the

Creator and the created. Thus, the Divine Authorship of the *Quran* remains a superbly undisputed fact. However, it would not be a blasphemy on our part to describe an intrinsically Divine Revelation as humane in its contents.

Man is the central figure in the *Quran*. Although essentially addressed to the Prophet Muhammad for the guidance of mankind, the *Quran* contains verses which are also directly addressed to the ubiquitous man. The significance of the *Quran* for humankind lies in the fact that while its contents relate to the social contexts of Mecca and Medina, it repeatedly enjoins upon man to mould his thought and behaviour on the pattern of Muhammad's and his companions' responses to the divine revelations. The responses of the prophets prior to Muhammad in the form of prayers, advice and admonitions are also specially noted in the *Quran* for the guidance of mankind. At the same time, however, innumerable verses in the *Quran* urge man to strive ceaselessly for the countenance (*ridha*) of Allah. Before we conclude, it needs to be stressed that our purpose is not to establish a kind of relationship with Allah that lies outside the *Sunna*, but it is an attempt to understand the *Quran* and the *Sunna* in the depths of our individual reason and love. Furthermore, a note of caution is also necessary. *Din* for us is a matter of attitudes, of perceptions, of feeling, of responses, of impulses, of inner strivings and above all, of moulding our individual acts in social relations in accordance with our ever-growing religious consciousness. Also, *din* is not simply a matter of theology, a particularity being the very negation of religious universality, but rather a matter of yearning to know the ultimate Reality through our own conduct. As Pickthall observes, even from "a Prophet's standpoint, theology is childish nonsense, the very opposite of religion, and its enemy; religion, for the Prophet, being not a matter of conjecture and speech, but of fact and conduct."[11] Theoretically speaking, we are fully conscious of our obligations as an integral part of the *umma*, but in actual practice, we are equally deeply conscious of our duties as individuals to Allah and the society we live in. On the Day of Judgment, we will be responsible for our personal actions in relation to the society which we live in rather than for our collective behaviour. It is our firm belief that our good deeds and sins will be weighed in relation to us as individuals rather than "us" as a collectivity.

Indeed, our reckoning at the personal level will start from the very moment we will return unto Him. Allah will punish us or reward us for our personal deeds on the Day of Judgment.

Ours is thus a personal attempt at understanding the *Quran*. Our purpose, then, is not to produce a replica of Mecca and Medina for, we are, by no stretch of the imagination, capable of attaining to the heights of the splendour and glory of the mission that saw fruition in the lifetime of the perfect man. The *Sunna* of Muhammad is a model for us. It provides us keys for understanding the *Quran* mainly as a Book of Guidance for our individual development. Our purpose is not to establish an Islamic state in the modern sense, for, we believe that the *Quran* has no political overtones. Nothing would be more blasphemous than to use an intrinsically divine Book of Guidance for the furtherance of our political objectives rooted in our various particular geographical environments. The *Quran's* message is universal rather than particular. It would be an intellectual disaster to propose the unity of humankind at the political level to people living in varied geographical and cultural environments; rather the *Quran* has historically asserted, and will continue to assert, their particular identities. But it is not unthinkable to talk in terms of the unity of mankind at the spiritual and intellectual levels. Since Allah's appeal is primarily to the intellect or the reason of ever-searching and sensitive souls, this explains the abiding relevance of the Book of Guidance in all situations or periods of history, aptly described as 'fleeting time'[12] in the *Quran*.

Notes and References

1. As a thoughtful reader of the *Quran* for nearly two decades, I have immensely benefited from the translations and exegesis of Shaikh al-Hind Mahmud al-Hasan, Maulana Ashraf 'Ali Thanwi, and Allama Yusuf Ali. The translations of Pickthall, Arberry and the exegesis of Maulana Muhammad Shafi together with that of Maulana Abul Ala Maududi helped me to develop my ideas in comparative perspectives over the years. I have read only the relevant portions from Maulana Azad's commentary on the *Quran*.
2. *Quran*, 2/2. "But to those who receive Guidance, He increases their guidance, and bestows on them their piety and restraint (from evil)". Ibid., 47/17.

3. Ibid., 3/64.
4. Ibid., 11/118.
5. Ibid., 9/13.
6. Ibid., 10/57-58.
7. Ibid., 16/36; 10/47. At another place: "And we never sent a messenger save with the language of his folk... ." Ibid., 14/4.
8. For the author's response to Kenneth Cragg "Minority predicament", See *Journal of Muslim Minority Affairs*, Vol. XII, No: I, Jan., London 1991, pp. 172-74.
9. The concept of the "Perfect Man" developed by 'Abd al-Karim al-Jili (d. 832/1428) in his well known work *al-Insan al-kamil*, though based on the Unity of Being *(Wahdat al-Wujud)* of Ibn Arabi (b. 560/1165), is not in conflict with the *Quran's* fundamental idea of the Universality of the spirit of human bodies. But the question remains whether man is profoundly conscious of his 'purgative ascent' out of matter. Whatever the misconceptions generally associated with this concept, the Prophet Muhammad has always remained the model of *insan-i-kamil* for even such Sufis as were erroneously supposed to have transgressed the *Shari'a*.
10. Abu Lahab, "Father of Flame", was the nickname of the arch enemy of Islam. The Quranic verses "Perish the hands of the Father of Flame! Perish he! No profit to him from all his wealth, and all his gains! Burnt soon will he be in a fire of blazing flame!..." *(Quran*, 111/1-3) proved to be prophetic when Abu Lahab himself perished and was "consumed with grief and his own fiery passion" following the defeat of the "leaders of persecution" at Badr.
11. Pickthall, *The Glorious Koran*, preface.
12. *Quran*, 75/20; 76/27.

2

CONVERSION TO ISLAM

The *Quran* is the final word of Allah and so is the finality of the prophethood of Muhammad *(khatam-i-nubbuwwat)* an undisputed fact. The Islamic belief about the *Quran's* immutability and historicity is nearly fourteen centuries old. The revelation of the *Quran* during a period of over 22 years in the social milieu of Mecca and Medina was itself the unfolding of an epoch-making event in the annals of world history. The *Quran* is neither dogmatic nor doctrinal but relational. It intrinsically serves to indicate, suggest and, above all, guide spiritual and social relations in an integrated whole embodying this world and the Hereafter. The concept of Islam as perfect *din* saw fruition in the evolution of a morally vibrant society under the leadership of Muhammad. Such a society was the result of the individual's behavioural response to the Quranic verses revealed to the Prophet suiting a particular social context, his sayings *(hadith)*, and deeds *(Sunna)*. While the Prophet's *Sunna* became a model for every Muslim, the Islamic society of his days became an ideal. It is both the model and ideal of the Prophet and his society respectively that have continued to inspire Muslims worldwide.

Conversion to Islam, culminating in the perfection of *din* in relation to the emulation of the model behaviour of the Prophet Muhammad and emergence of an ideal society, was essentially varied. The first type of human response to the divine message was characterised by self-discipline, self-abnegation, self-effacement, self-sacrifice, self-control and self-evident submission of the early followers of Islam. They cast themselves in the mould of the model and were converts in the strict religious, volitional and intellectual sense. They were companions of the Prophet, always ready to sacrifice their life and wealth at his call. They were dynamic individuals making their presence felt in the evolving *umma* as true servants of Allah. Islam owes its perfection to their incessant struggle and tribulations for orienting their conduct in accordance with the model. The distinguishing trait of their individual and social behaviour was submission to Allah and His human messenger in all respects. Islam thus came to signify not only human submission to Allah but obedience to the leader *(imam)*.

It follows that unity of belief, of purpose and of action was at the root of the evolution of a morally vibrant society. Unshakeable belief in Allah's unity *(tawhid)* and the converts' consciousness *(sha'ur)*, particularly at the individual level, to do what was morally right were the sinews of the ideal society. Oneness forms the core of basic Islamic teachings. Allah is one, His last messenger is one, and a true believer is one in the sense that he alone is responsible for his actions. Islam thus appears to me not a matter of theological definition but a historical fact worthy of inner realisation, first at the individual and then at the social level. The divine, prophetic and a believer's individuality or identity are all different yet unitive aspects of the same idea of Allah's unity. The intellectual merit of this idea of unity is to reflect ceaselessly on our own human existence in relation to the Creator, His last messenger's spiritio-historic mission and, of course, our own responses in the light of the past and simultaneously in the hope of our assured future in the eternal abode *(akhira)*.

The society that emerged under the leadership of the Prophet Muhammad, although ideal in the strictest sense, could not destroy the forces arrayed against it. If, on the one hand, the Prophet's uncle, Abu Lahab, subjected his nephew and his followers to all kinds of persecutions, on the other, there were converts within the ideal society itself who were condemned as hypocrites in the *Quran*.[1] Apparently they did not lag behind the first category of believers in respect of observance of fundamentals of faith; yet their conversion was not sincere. Hence such epithets for them as *munafiqin*,[2] *mushrikin*,[3] *mufsidin*[4] recur in the *Quran* according to the degree of their obsessional behaviour to transgress the intelligible norms set by the model behaviour of the Prophet. This category of hypocrites, which is described in the *Quran* as "plunged into error"[5] is poles apart from the one that always strives to ward off all that is "evil".

The very dynamic of a Muslim society is rooted in the inherent human tendency of its members to digress. The *Quran* exemplifies the inner dynamic of human society in the following words:

> Let there arise out of you a community of people who invite to goodness, and enjoin right conduct and forbid what is wrong; such are the ones to achieve happiness.[6]

The emphasis is on invitation (*da'wah*) rather than force. The verse is of central importance considering the historicity and universality of its context and relevance. It calls for tolerance in the face of intolerance. It urges a never-ceasing struggle at the individual and societal level for overcoming the forces of evil by way of precept and example rather than by force. And but for their fortitude, members of the evolving ideal society under the leadership of Muhammad would not have migrated from Mecca to Medina under very trying conditions. What is of further significance to note is the absence of the use of force on the eve of the conquest of Mecca under the command of the Prophet. The conquest of Mecca was not an act of superior arms over inferior ones, but it was, in essence, the victory of a moral and spiritual force over a strong enemy. It was the historic vindication of a spiritual and social force over self-indulgent, self-seeking, self-willed, self-centred and self-absorbed forces.

Did Islam put an end to the ethnocentricity of the tribal Arabs? Although history provides an affirmative answer to this question, yet my musings on the events of early Islamic history focus the mind on a problem that had serious implications for Islam. How is it that Islam's worst enemies have been (and continue to be) found amongst the ranks of the Muslims themselves? Who killed three of the pious *Khulafa*? Was it the "accursed" Jew, Christian or Muslim? The fact is that conversion of a certain category of Arabs to Islam, though a matter of publicly approved attitudes, beliefs and principles was in reality nothing short of subversion of attempts towards the emulation of model and ideal. Wasn't the subversive psyche of the hypocritical category of converts also responsible for the tragedy of Karbala? True, the martyrdom of the grandsons of the Prophet revived the spirit of *jihad* in the context of model and ideal, but didn't the brutal massacre of the Prophet's family at the hands of none other than men professing Islam confirm the Quranic view about the degrees of conversion or faith?

Let us now turn our attention to the conversion of the Bedouin tribes. The *Quran* categorizes assimilation of the desert Arabs in Islam during Muhammad's time as far from complete or total:

> The desert Arabs say, 'we believe,' say, ye have no faith; but (only) say, 'we have submitted our wills to Allah.' For not yet has faith entered your hearts....[7]

Here a sociological question of crucial significance is worthy of consideration. The dichotomy of behavioural response to Islam is clearly indicated. Islam first appeared in an urban environment. Mecca was the hub of commercial and intellectual activities. By the standards of time, it was a flourishing city and an entrepot for the caravan trade. Notwithstanding the primitiveness and permissiveness characterising the consciousness of the *asabiyyah*[8] of various tribal groups, there was ample scope and opportunity for discussion and creativity in *jahilyya*.[9] And but for this, the *jahilyya* would not have been synchronous with the level of the high-watermark reached by the Arabic poetry. There was no dearth of men of intellect among Christians and Jews in spite of their adherence to their respective distorted traditions. Islam's main achievement lay in synthesizing the diverse tribal ethics of the Arabs into a state of unity and universality. The intensity of the debate that arose in response to *Tawhidic Weltanschuung* in the first instance may appear surprising to many. But Islam's ability to penetrate both the intellect and heart of the wrangling Arabs during the emergence of the ideal society testifies to the high standard of culture, education and training set by the Prophet for assimilating the Arabs into Islam. In this respect it was not only *jihad* against the baser instincts of the self or soul but also against the snares of human intellect that was laid down as a necessary condition for conversion to Islam in the strict religious sense. Did not such an incessant struggle against the enemy within become the keynote of the Companions of the Prophet? Was not such a continuous struggle of the soul and intellect behind the progress of the expanding frontiers of Islamic civilisation?

An objective understanding of Islam therefore postulates not a sudden conversion on our part within the parameters of the first category of converts but demands the widening of our intellectual understanding to feel vicariously the historical experience of the Companions. The heart of the matter is to overcome the intellectual error of confining one's reason within the bounds of temporal and terrestrial experience. But when human reasoning is anchored in the Mind of the *Quran,* one is certain to feel it working in symbiosis. Let me therefore elaborate on the Quranic degrees of conversion or faith.

The *Quran* mentions three states or stages as a prerequisite for the spiritual development of an individual: (i) *Ammara*[10] which is inclined to evil and, if not kept under check, will utterly ruin the soul; (ii) *Lawwama*[11] which is self-reproaching and seeks God's grace and pardon after repentance and hopes to reach salvation, and (iii) *Mutma'inna,*[12] the exalted stage of all, 'when it achieves full rest and satisfaction.

During the days of my youth I was greatly moved by a remark made by Dr. Karan Singh, son of the last Maharaja of Kashmir. In an interview granted to the editor of an Urdu digest[13], he was asked about his ambition in life. The princely philosopher answered, "My desire is to know the truth about the soul." For over two decades now, I have been doing a great deal of soul-searching to discover what truth the human soul can unfold about itself. But in this continuous search the only truth revealed to me, again and again, has been that the human soul was made to walk erect and straight in the hope of achieving that noble ambition which is natural to the mind of man. The saddest of all failures is that of a mind that does not aspire to discover its soul; and worse still is the failure of the soul to establish a meaningful nexus with the human mind.

It follows that there is a basic relationship between man's mind and soul. Fundamentally religion deprecates any attempt at compartmentalising reason into the sacred and the profane. The legacy of the Renaissance and Protestant movements in Western Europe was an exaggerated emphasis on the triumph of reason over faith or, in other words, the triumph of rationality of the human mind over the irrationality of the human soul. Consequently, the West lost its soul but regained the worldly power that it appeared to have been losing before the Renaissance occurred. But, in its triumphant march, the West forgot that while pushing religion to the background in everyday affairs, it actually and seriously wounded its own soul. Divested of soul in the sense I have been using the word here, and empowered with what is miscalled civilisation, the State in the West became an engine of oppression. The spiritual bankruptcy of the soulless began to work in several directions. The result was not only compartmentalisation but also vulgarisation of human knowledge. The spiritual ethics were tabooed and Protestant ethics with emphasis on the progressive development of material civilisation became the watchword of the new polity cut off from the Church of Rome. Individualism, a moral principle especially typical of Protestant ideology and ethics, emerged as a potent force. With the evolution of capitalist society emerged the belief in the policy of extending a country's power base and influence in the world through diplomacy or military force, and especially by acquiring colonies. Imperialism and monopoly capitalism became the hallmarks of Western civilisation.

From the standpoint of the *Quran,* the progress of Western civilisation needs to be studied in terms of the first stage of man's development. Such terms as spirituality, secrets of the soul or immorality of the soul appear meaningless to me if not studied in relation to the condition of the human spirit in its social environments. What is of significance to enquire is whether the *nafs* or soul is enmeshed in *ammara* or *lawwama*. Neither soul nor matter can exist in a vacuum. What, indeed, has led to the existence of such belief is the human error made on the logical and intellectual plane by dogmatising the idea of soul within the narrow limits of ideological spheres. The *Quran,* however, describes this world as a training place for the immortality of human soul.[14] Did not Allah breathe His spirit into the matter?[15] Did not He make Adam from clay? What was the divine wisdom (*hikma*) behind creating Adam of clay and not solely out of His own spirit?

Matter and soul are interrelated objective realities. So long as soul remains active, matter remains animated. But the moment the soul departs from matter, the human body is reduced to a corpse and starts to decompose. It is buried or cremated and in either case the earth absorbs its own earth. The reality of the world of matter ends before our own eyes. Divine chemistry

causes matter to reunite with matter but this apparent reality
does not open our eyes to the actual unreality of this world.
Viewed in this perspective, the absorption of the soul in timeless
unicity after death is comprehensible. So long as the soul lives in
the world, it undergoes various experiences. But it is the
enlightened soul alone which strives. It receives ripples from the
moment of its descent on this planet to that of its return to Him.
Every human being, irrespective of his religious, political or
ideological affiliations, has a soul. Without the soul the world
cannot exist; there would be no singing of birds, no humming of
bees, no sonorous voice of the *mu'azzin* in the mosque or ringing
of bells in the churches or temples, had God created the world
soulless. The reality and unreality of the soul and the world
respectively are relative; neither the world nor the soul can exist
irrespective of each other. Perhaps the following verse of the
Quran quenches our quest for the truth about the soul.

> Had God not driven back the people, some by the means of
> others, there had been destroyed cloisters and churches,
> oratories and mosques, wherein God's Name is much
> mentioned. Assuredly God will help him who helps Him—
> surely God is All-Strong, All-mighty—who, if We establish
> them in the land, perform the prayer, and pay the alms, and
> bid to honour, and forbid dishonour; and unto God belongs
> the issue of all affairs.[16]

The *Quran* allows freedom to the individual to train his soul
according to its injunctions; or to improverish it by utter
negligence. The greatest sin, from the standpoint of the *Quran*, in
striking contrast to the Biblical belief, is not the inborn sinfulness
of man but his ignorance. And what breeds ignorance is the habit
of negligence towards the training of the soul. Did not each
individual in "the posterity of Adam" have a separate existence
from the time of Adam?" Didn't Allah take a Covenant from
mankind long before the creation of this world? Isn't the
Covenant binding on each human soul? Since the Covenant of
every individual human being before Allah awakens a seeker to
the sublime supremacy, the dangers, the accountableness, and
the glorious stations of the immortal soul, it would therefore be of
immense value for our own souls to reflect on the following
verses:

> And (remember) when thy Lord brought forth from the children of Adam, from their reins, their seed, and made them testify of themselves, (saying): Am I not your Lord? They said: Yea, verily. We testify. (That was) lest ye should say at the day of Resurrection: Lo! of this we were unaware;

> Or lest ye should say: (It is) only (that) our fathers ascribed partners to Allah of old and we were (their) seed after them. Wilt Thou destroy us on account of that which those who follow falsehood did? Thus we detail Our revelation, that they may return.[17]

Our imperfect faculty of reason may not be prepared to accept the eternal fact about our primary obligation to establish a purposeful relationship with our suppressed soul. But the souls of the righteous, on awakening, travel a long way in feeling the eternal truth of the Covenant. And those souls who constantly endeavour to have an understanding *(ma'rifa)* of the Reality *(haqqiqa)* are enlightened ones. Most of them are at the self-reproaching stage *(lawwama)* seeking Allah's grace and pardon after repentance to hopefully earn His countenance *(ridha)*, and only a few reach the final stage in the journey of their soul *(mutma'inna)*. About such great souls the *Quran* remarks:

> O soul at peace return unto the Lord, well-pleased, well-pleasing! Enter thou among my servants! Enter thou My Paradise.[18]

The last stage typifies the radiant personality of the man of God. Without the existence of such souls not only the world but even religion would have ended in an abyss. As Emerson says: "We are much better believers in immortality than we can give grounds for,—The real evidence is too subtle, or is higher than we can write down in proportions." Nevertheless, the mystic poet of Islam, Maulana Jalaluddin Rumi, reminds us of the human soul in ennobled attitude:

> The man of God is drunken without wine,
> The man of God is full without meat,
> The man of God is distraught and bewildered,
> The man of God has no food or sleep.
> The man of God is a king, 'neath the dervish-cloak,

The man of God is a treasure in a ruin.
The man of God is not of air and earth,
The man of God is not of fire and water,
The man of God is a boundless sea,
The man of God rains pearls without a cloud,
The man of God hath hundred moons and skies,
The man of God hath hundred suns,
The man of God is not learned from book,
The man of God is made wise by the Truth,
The man of God is beyond infidelity and religion,
To the man of God right and wrong are alike,
The man of God has ridden away from Not-being,
The man of God is gloriously attended,
The man of God is concealed, Shamsi Din;
The man of God do thou seek and find.[19]

But the great majority of human beings prefer to live in a world of their own making. Such people are not devoid of introspection. However, their thinking is restricted to the events of the temporal world. Mundane affairs clog their thinking: if they do not become conscious of their obsessional and wayward disposition, their souls are ultimately ruined. They become soulless. And it is the soullessness of souls which not only destroys intellect but also the world. Shouldn't the fate of Communism versus Capitalism in our own days send ripples to the soul of the soulless? The poet-philosopher of the Indian subcontinent, Allama Mohammad Iqbal, though profoundly conscious of Karl Marx's contribution to history and humanity, was simultaneously not oblivious of the abject poverty of such a human soul. In a terse verse he describes Marx as *Kalim-i-bay Tajalli*, i.e., the one who, in spite of his ability to communicate a message, is without inner light.

Having studied the nature of conversion to Islam in relation to the soul, mind and society, it would appear that the human soul cannot afford to remain stationary. But this is not true of the soul of the soulless. It stagnates for want of training and ultimately ruins itself by inaction. Since there exists no positive relationship between the soul of the soulless and the human mind, the latter gains ascendancy over the former. But the supremacy of the mind over the soul is relative in that the mind is not independent of life situations. The society and mind in fact enter into an effective dialogue with one another and this reciprocal pull results in the birth of an ideology.

Ideology belongs to the realm of mind and not religion. No ideology is universally valid since it is essentially rooted in the mundane affairs of the world. Although the Western reason avowedly triumphed over faith, yet the Western mind could not produce a universal ideology. Instead, the birth of conflicting ideologies in the West in the wake of the triumphant march of reason only served to terrorise, vulgarise and divide the world. Secularism, atheism, rationalism, Marxism, capitalism, liberalism, fascism, fundamentalism and so on are ideological constructs of the Western mind.

Nationalism was the child of the French Revolution. Although the French Revolution stood for liberty, equality and fraternity, yet it did not make a landmark in the history of mankind without shedding human blood. Thousands of human lives were lost as a result of such bloody events as the French, American, Russian and Chinese revolutions. Did these revolutions forge any global unity? How many wars were fought in the name of nationalism in Western Europe? And, worse of all, how many countries were colonised by the civilised West in the name of ideology? The legacy of colonisation of Asian and Middle Eastern countries is too well known to merit any elaboration. Suffice it to say, continued instability in South Asia and West Asia is attributable to the ideological imperialism of the West. Behind the occurrence of the two World Wars, also, worked ideological factors. The United Nations came into being with the avowed intention of forging peace in the world. But the ideology of peace also proved to be deceptive or elusive. For many years the UN's peace efforts were hampered by the differing ideologies of the two world powers. But when Washington's ideology triumphed over that of the Communist Soviet Union, the United States began to talk in terms of creating a new world order. But the hopes generated towards the fulfilment of that goal have been belied by the double standards applied by the West in the case of Iraq and Bosnia Herzegovina.

What contributes to disorder and instability in the world order? Is it religion or the human mind? Marx called religion the opium of the people. But that perception was based on the history of Western Europe. In the West, religion had corrupted the minds of the people since the human mind had corrupted it. Hence the revolt against corrupt religion was inevitable; but the revolt assumed such dangerous proportions that religion now came to be equated with fear and ignorance. Religion was no longer seen as an integrative force, but the source of superstitions, preconceived and false notions. The Renaissance and Reformation movements heralded the modern age. With the disintegration of medieval society, a new spirit of scientific enquiry stressing the practical function of thought replaced the so-called theoretical contemplation of a hierarchical and sacred world. The concept of ideology first emerged in the West as a critique of religion in close connection with both political practice and the development of science. As Jorge Larrain observes: "In the feudal society ideology resorted to religion in order to justify class domination; in capitalist society it appears as science so as to conceal all trace of class domination."[20] In either case ideology gives a sort of legitimacy to the dominant class. Whether it is the ideological concept of uprooting the dominance of the priestly classes or that of imposing the dictatorship of the proletariat or that of advocating the claim of making science or scientific process itself an ideology—in fact, all such conceptions are rooted in the sustained attempts at perpetuating the ideology of absolute dominance of the rational mind. No wonder, then, that all efforts at creating a new world order sound hollow.

Ideology is theoretically definitive and historically conditioned. It is a system of ideas that form the basis of an economic or political theory or that are held by a particular group or persons. Our ideologies differ since they express the interests of varied groups, parties and nations. Hence the question that arises is whether faith is ideology.

Faith denotes prior recognition of something as true without proof. Faith in the supernatural (God, angels, devils, spirits, the next world, the Day of Judgment, etc.) is an essential part of Semitic religions. The belief that all natural objects and phenomena (e.g., trees, stones, the wind, etc.) have souls is called animism. The transmigration of souls and incarnation is also a matter of faith. But faith is not dogmatic considering the fact that it basically involves voluntary surrender of the self to an unknown power. But, in the context of the *Quran*, faith assumes qualitative significance when it distinguishes between mere faith and reasoned faith.[21]

From the standpoint of the Quran, Islam is the primordial faith of mankind. The necessity for reviving it arose at frequent intervals in history in that its *tawhidic* spirit was either eroded or undermined by the very faith of the man in blind faith. Belief in a god, or multiple deities, or goddesses, often carved in stones and used as objects of worship, belongs to the category of blind faith. Similarly trees, rivers, springs assume the character of idols if made objects of worship. The image of Christ carved out of stone was antithetical to the very spirit of monotheism enshrined in the *Bible* and mentioned in the *Quran*. Hence it was not the faith of Christ but blind adoration of the person of Christ by his followers that was questioned. Idolisation is condemned in the *Quran* because it involves blind adoration of the object personified. The practice of religious idolatry gives birth to cults. In sociological terms, a cult is a group having a sacred ideology and a set of rites centring around their sacred symbols. Cult is also interpreted as a religion that is considered or held to be false or 'unorthodox'.

Neither an ideology nor a cult, Islam claims perfection in the historical context of Muhammad's and his followers historic response to the divine message. At no stage in history could Muslim behaviour reach or go beyond the standard of perfection or excellence that Islam achieved during the time of the Prophet. Notwithstanding the emergence of cults and ideologies during a chequered course of Muslim history, it is important to remember that the revitalisation movements in Muslim societies checked their growth to such an extent that they were reduced to the position of insignificance. Islam, in fact, has had and continues to have, an indefatigable resilience to overcome the fissiparous tendencies of cults or ideologies. This is reflected in the never-ceasing endeavour of the faithful to strive for what is deemed to be worthy of imitation. The Islamic ideal is not a concept or standard of perfection existing merely in the imagination. It sets a pattern for moulding the personality of the believer into the historic model and ideal.

Notes and References

1. *Quran*, 2/4; 3/167-168; 4/60-63; 4/141-143; 9/64-65; 9/67-69; 4/71-73 etc.
2. Ibid., "When the hypocrites come to thee, they say, 'We bear witness that thou art indeed the messenger of Allah'. Yea, Allah knoweth

that thou art indeed His messenger. And Allah beareth witness that
hypocrites are indeed liars" (Ibid., 63/1). The hypocrites have been
condemned in the *Quran* for their double-dealing. "They swear by
Allah that they said nothing (evil), but indeed they uttered
blasphemy, and they uttered it after accepting Islam..." (Ibid., 9/74).

3.   One who associates others with God in His divinity is a *mushrik*.
Although the term has been invariably used in the *Quran* for the
pagan Arabs, believers have been repeatedly warned against *shirk*
"...to associate others with God is the highest wrong-doing" (Ibid.,
31/13).

4.   "There is the type of man whose speech about this world's life may
dazzle thee, and he calls Allah to witness about what is in his heart;
yet is the most contentious of enemies. When he turns his back, his
aim everywhere is to spread mischief through the earth and destroy
crops and progeny. But Allah loves not mischief. (Ibid., 2/204-205).
For "corruption on the earth", see Ibid., 2/11; 27, 205; 7/56, 85; 11/
16; 12/73; 13/25; 16/88;26/152 etc. ".... and seek not (occasions for)
mischief in the land: for Allah loves not those who do mischief."
(Ibid., 28/77).

5.   "But their brethren (the evil ones) plunge them deeper into error,
and never relax (their efforts)" (Ibid., 7/202).

6.   Ibid., 3/104.

7.   Ibid., 49/14. The wandering Arabs were more or less lukewarm in
their faith. While Islam demands complete submission of one's
being to Allah, the wandering Arabs were found wanting in faith on
account of the pettiness of their hearts and minds. While in the
above verse the context is the Banu Asad, "who came to profess
Islam in order to get charity during famine," at another place (Ibid.,
48/11-15) their failings have been described in terms of "false
excuse based on a calculation of worldly profit and loss!"

8.   Islam cut at the roots of tribal unity based on group feelings and
solidarity *(asabiyah)*. Under the dynamic leadership of the Prophet
Muhammad it gave a different orientation to such cohesive forces
for keeping society together on *Tawhidic Weltanschuung*.

9.   The period of ignorance in Arabia before the advent of the *Quran*.

10.   Ibid., 12/53.

11.   Ibid., 5/2.

12.   Ibid., 89/27.

13.   Probably it was the *Shabistan* Urdu digest published from Delhi.

14.   See *Quran*, 89/27-30.

15.   Ibid., 38/72; 15/29.

16.   Ibid., 20/40-41.

17.   Ibid., 9/172-174.

18.   Ibid., 89/27-30.

19. *Selections from Divani Shamsi Tabriz,* ed. R.A. Nicholson, Cambridge, first paperback edition, 1977, pp. 28-31.

20. Jorge Larrain, *The Concept of Ideology,* first Indian edition, Bombay, 1980, p. 211.

21. The Arabic term for faith is *iman.* It literally means "to know", "to believe" and "to be convinced beyond the least shadow of doubt". Thus Maulana Abul ala Maududi rightly observes that faith "is firm belief arising out of knowledge and conviction". *Towards Understanding Islam,* Trans. and edited by Khurshid Ahmed, Markazi Maktaba Jamat-i-Islami Hind (Delhi, 6th edition, 1967), p. 24. However, it must be emphasized that such a kind of faith is preceded by believing or having faith in what is unknown called *iman-bilghaib.* Since the "faith in the unknown" commits a true believer to an ethic of action, this is the reason that the *Quran* stresses the importance of intellect and reason in leading a purposeful existence in a spiritio-historical context.

3

THE SPIRITUAL AND HISTORICAL FOUNDATIONS OF THE *QURAN*

We have seen that Islam and the world are not two independent categories in that both owe their existence to Allah. From the standpoint of the *Quran*, neither Islam nor the world can transcend one another. The transitory world was created as *dar al-amal* for the next world or Hereafter which is eternal. Hence, the man who realises the basic truth about the impermanence of this world seeks to condition his thought and behaviour in such a manner as may not bring him in conflict with either his religious or everyday affairs. The ability to recognise this world's transitoriness is rare. And an indepth comprehension of this eternal fact marks the beginning of spiritual awareness. Viewed against this formulation, the ambition of conquering the world appears futile. And even if a particular nation succeeds in conquering a major portion of the globe, its ascendancy cannot continue for long. As a matter of fact, the limits of human reason as well as the widening horizons of material and technological progress themselves create conditions for the destruction of the supremacy of a particular system, ideology or the so-called world or superpower.

Although the *Quran* and history bear testimony to the rise and fall of nations, yet Muslims generally seem to be unmindful of the nature of the ebb and flow of the intensity of the historical process. The Muslims' persistent belief that they were once a great power and now they are not so points to something wrong in their thinking, rather than in their history. This belief has almost attained the force of law in the apologetic writings on Islamic history. Little wonder, then, that various interpretations exist regarding the failure of Muslims or Islam to keep pace with history. The backwardness of Muslims *vis-a-vis* the scientific development of the West is explained in terms of the unchangeableness of the Islamic law *(Shari'a)* and consequent unquestioned adherence to tradition, and above all, the inability of the Muslim religious leadership to direct worldly affairs. Most of these explanations, though grounded in reason, are not wholly true. The heavens would not have fallen had Muslims achieved progress in the field of science commensurate with the West since the Industrial Revolution. While the West emerged as an ideological force following rapid strides in science and technology, this development did not undermine the strength of Islam as a spiritual force as it did in respect of Christianity. It is tempting to ask whether Islam would have retained its spiritual potential had its adherents dedicated themselves solely to the pursuit of material development.

The very idea of the Muslim obsession with the past glory of Islam seems to be a jigsaw puzzle. Muslims feel proud of their ancestors' contribution to science, yet they do not have a true and perceptive sense of their failure to inherit an ancestral scientific legacy. They proudly prate about the strength of the great Muslim generals in subjugating kingdoms and empires, yet they find themselves helpless and desperate against their adversaries in the absence of the like of such heroes. They talk a great deal about Islam's glorious success during the time of the Prophet Muhammad and *Khilafat-i-Rashida*, yet they vacillate between fulfilling the requirements of the model behaviour of their beloved Prophet and that of the so-called "Islamic ideology". Islam is as worthy of emulation as it was when the Prophet delivered his last sermon, yet Muslims give proof of their inability to understand the eternity of his message for mankind.

The message brought by Muhammad in the form of the *Quran* was simple rather than twisted. The *Quran* is the final word of Allah for mankind. Muhammad was the 'Seal of the Prophets' who had been sent before for guiding humanity, and the Author of the *Quran*, as the sole Nourisher *(Rabb)* of several worlds, alone deserves adoration. One does not need special study of Islamic jurisprudence *(fiqh)*, Islamic spirituality *(tasawwuf)*, Islamic law *(Shari'a)*, and the so-called "Islamic ideology" to understand the pristine truth of the message enshrined in the *Quran* and exemplified in the Prophet Muhammad's behaviour. The understanding of Islam and even the intellect itself are impaired if one begins one's study of Islam with works aimed at either conceptualising or ideologising Islam. So I would suggest a common sense approach to Islam for the one who is inquisitive to know the truth about the "claims" made by Allah rather than by His followers. I shun the traditional theological approach because it dogmatises Islam notwithstanding its academic merit for those who are already in the field.

Allah created the world with Adam as His vicegerent on this planet. All children of Adam have been vouchsafed vicegerency. The only issue, in my opinion, that divides the children of Adam is whether they are prepared to accept the exalted office of vicegerency of Allah. Since the acceptance of this honour demands inner striving and fortitude on the part of man, this is the reason that very few people are prepared to struggle in His way. But this is not the whole truth. Most men are by nature inclined to know and understand their Creator. However, their quest for knowledge of the truth is lost in the dispersion of interest resulting from vagueness of their thinking. And what blurs one's understanding of the Creator is not one's inability, but the ability to perceive the Creator the other way.

The other way is not the Creator's way. The Creator's way is straight and not tedious. But man's thinking makes it so. The primordial religion that the Creator sent to the world was simple and natural. All prophets appealed to common sense because of their common sense approach to the problems of everyday life. The necessity for reviving the pristine spirit of religion arose time and again which is why the *Quran* makes mention of several prophets who were sent for the guidance of mankind. In fact, each nation had a prophet.[1] All prophets, according to the *Quran,* taught the oneness of the Nourisher *(Rabb).* But enough of man's ignorance about his Creator could not be completely dispelled since man chose to deviate from the Straight Path. He made his own gods and goddesses. His belief in the divinity of the sun, moon, winds, rivers, trees, snakes, mountains, fire, idols of stones and wood, was the result of his misguided quest. The belief in local deities was fostered by the ties of kinship and the sense of belonging to a particular tribe and cult. Although the prophets of Judaism and Christianity laid stress on the oneness of God, their followers departed from true belief and made religion a handiwork of dogmas.

The *Quran* was revealed to the last of the prophets[2] for two reasons of vital significance. First, the divine books sent before the *Quran* had lost credibility in that the human reason of theologians had led to several interpolations in the original texts. The *Quran* prescribed laws in the light of social issues that came up before the Prophet Muhammad. Such laws were not totally new, for it would have meant a radical departure from previous injunctions. In fact, the Quranic injunctions were comprehensively new in orientation and spirit rather than content. How can Allah be contradictory? He cannot say one thing today and another tomorrow. Of course, evidence to the contrary might be cited from the *Quran* itself by its detractors. Such evidence, however, relates not to the fundamentals of faith but to certain issues of lesser importance.

Second, the Quranic revelations may be described as a divine response to the spiritual and human urges of the most perfect among human beings. The *Quran* was not revealed in just a fraction of a second or a moment. And if such had been the case there would have been no need for struggle in history. A moment's divine operation would have gone like clockwork. Allah was (and is) superbly capable of stabilising the world both with perfect regularity and precision. But the essence of the *Quran* is that it is not Islam but its adherents who are on trial in this unstable world. This is why a Muslim's entire lifespan is marked by the spirit of inner striving for the greater and relative good in this world and the Hereafter. It would not, therefore, be difficult to understand why the *Quran* was revealed in parts during a course of nearly twenty-three years of the continuous struggle of the Prophet against the atrophy of the Arab society.

The response of Allah to Muhammad's strivings and the consequent response of the Prophet to His commands was an inextricably divinely-oriented social process. The process began as a result of the desire of human heart to know the Creator in a society characterised by worship of hundreds of idols. At no stage in the evolution of his religious career, before the revelation of the *Quran*, had Muhammad himself worshipped idols. Instead, he had sought his Creator in solitude. His contemplation ultimately brought him close to the Creator who exalted[3] and immortalised his name by bestowing upon him special grace in the form of the *Quran*, Divine audience on the eve of ascension *(mi'raj)* and unparalleled honour in being the last Prophet of mankind.

For arriving at an understanding of Islam, our common sense demands some understanding of the *Quran*, of *mi'raj* and of the finality of the prophethood of Muhammad.

Ever since portions of the revealed knowledge were compiled during the period of the third Caliph, Uthman, the Quran has retained its incorruptible original character. There have been no interpolations, not even a scintilla of doubt among Muslims since the demise of the Prophet over the authenticity of the Quranic verses. The two major divisions among Muslims— Sunnis and Shias—have always accepted the unquestionable authenticity and infallibility of the *Quran*. And if there exists any difference between the two it relates to the interpretation rather than the contents of the *Quran* in addition to the latter-day developments in Islamic history. It is true that during the time of the Prophet the divine authorship of the *Quran* was disputed by the disbelievers. Being 'connoisseurs of language and rhetoric', however, the pagan poets failed to produce even a few verses comparable with those contained in the *Quran*[4]. This objective fact was no less a miracle and has since remained an evident proof for accepting the *Quran* as the source of mother of Scripture *(Umm al-kitab)*[5]. Muslim tradition and history are full of stories concerning individual conversions to Islam on hearing its inimitable message. Umar, the second caliph, owed his entry into Islam to the *Quran's* powerful impact upon his mind in the wake of his sister's conversion. She was engaged in the recitation of the Quran when she found Umar, feared among the pagan Arabs for his belligerence, at her doorstep. Fearing sacrilege at the hands of her infuriated brother, she hid parts of the *Quran*. But even in a state of anger Umar was overwhelmed when his sister began to recite verses from the *Quran* at her brother's command.

That the *Quran* has had a profound influence on the lives of millions of individuals for nearly fourteen hundreds years is an undisputed historical fact rather than the perpetuated myth of an ancient lore. The sublime effect of its message on the human mind and behaviour cannot be felt in just one or two readings. Being essentially the Book of Guidance for mankind it needs constant reading, revision, memorisation, and above all, contemplation. Nor can its reading be finished in ordinary terms. The trouble with the best of Western minds has always been their enviable habit of reading with a critical mind for the sake of promoting knowledge, discussion and scientific enquiry. This method is not applicable to the *Quran* in that it sets a different criterion for furthering the cause of knowledge. Since the finite perceptions of the human mind fail to understand or contemplate all the aspects of spiritual and temporal life in totality, the Westerners like Thomas Carlyle are deluded by their own reasoning into believing that the *Quran* is "a wearisome, confused jumble, crude, incondite."

The *Quran* first appeals to the original uncorrupted nature of the human mind, heart and soul to accept it as the word of Allah. Reading the *Quran* as a man of reasoned faith and as that of the reasoned mind makes a world of difference. This difference is as elusive as the Hereafter appears to the reasoning mind. In the Quranic sense, faith begins with the birth and evolution of consciousness in the human mind about the eternal reality of this fleeting world. Once we have made a reading of the *Quran* on the basis of our faith in the Unseen, this very faith will open up new vistas of discovery and research. Thus faith in the Unseen and reflection on the verses sent down from heaven are the prerequisites for understanding the *Quran*. This lifelong exercise demands *sha'ur*[6], *tadabbur*[7] and *tafakkur*[8] on our part. In fact, the *Quran* repeatedly appeals to these essential qualities of the human mind for understanding its deeper meaning.[9] Once the human mind is able to develop the consciousness required by the *Quran*, its reasoning faculties would be moulded into clarity and maturity of vision, thought and behaviour. Reflection on the Quranic verses leads to an unending journey of spiritual import from darkness to Light.[10]

The deep and meaningful relationship between the esoteric and exoteric elements of the religious life of a believer is comprehensible only to such individuals as regard the recitation of the *Quran* the surest means of approach to Allah. This consciousness that unites the created with the Creator has to be understood in both emotional and intellectual terms. As a matter of fact, an outside observer can rarely have the equilibrium of emotional and intellectual attitudes demanded of a believer. In the context of the *Quran*, love and consciousness are born spontaneously on feeling or contemplating the pervading presence of divine reality while reading it. The key to understanding the depth of the *Quran's* eternal message is, therefore, inculcation of divine love in the heart with the growing consciousness of living, thinking and acting in His presence.

Contemplating the *Quran* does not mean engaging oneself in mere religious meditation and thoughfulness but also moulding our social behaviour in consonance with the essence of its teachings. The fundamental teaching of the *Quran* is not ethnocentric but universalist in belief. That is, there is no God but Allah who is the sole Nourisher of the Worlds. This eternal truth about the Creator has to be affirmed daily during the course of prayer in a state of thoughtful presence before Allah.

Prayer, then, is not a ritual in the ordinary sense but a duty. Each act during prayer springs from a sense of duty towards Allah and His creatures. The believer begins his prayer with words "Allah is Great" and concludes it with the yearning for His peace and grace for the world and its inhabitants. The Muslim's act of prayer is nothing short of the ascension of the man. The shared exalted ambition of being watched by Allah[11] through prayer is the vital nexus between believers.

The Prophet Muhammad's departure from the earth into heaven on a particular night is called *mi'raj*. The summit between the "Nourisher of the Worlds" and the "Grace of the Worlds" took place in a few seconds in our reckoning of time. Without going into the controversy whether *mi'raj* was a bodily transportation or mere movement of the spirit, the historical fact of spiritual import is the occurrence of the event itself. It was a unique kind of spiritual experience; hence not easily comprehensible to rationalists with their penchant for parading their discursive reason. Any explanation of spiritual experience demands not an ingrained disillusionment with religion but an inculcated and invigorated feeling of faith in one's spiritual being. How can the one who has become disenchanted with religion feel empathically or understand thoughtfully the spiritual experience of the unique and the highest kind? Unless one disencumbers oneself of the burden of one's own misguided reason, one would continue to remain disgusted with religion. This is why *mi'raj* has been treated casually in the Western Orientalist literature in striking contrast to the significance given to the migration *(hijra)* of the Prophet and his followers from Mecca to Medina. Since the migration of the victims of persecution connotes the struggle for survival and the gradual flowering of a religio-political community, it appeals to the Western reasoning mind. Notwithstanding the historic significance of *hijra* in the annals of Islam, the eternal importance of *mi'raj* in exalting the model of perfect human personality deserves some explanation.

Mystics belonging to various religions have always had spiritual experiences. But, apart from mystics, ordinary men have dream-like experiences which make them 'travel' in the past or future into a timeless time. Such dreams have been empirically corroborated and defy explanation. The biographical accounts of Muslim mystics are replete with various kinds of experiences. However, the unravelling of certain spiritual experiences has led to a great deal of controversy, as for example, the discussion that raged round the mystic experience of unity of existence *(wahdat al-wujud)* and unity of vision *(wahdat al-shuhud)*.[12] While these experiences remain outside the pale of history, yet Allama Muhammad Iqbal draws a neat distinction between the experience of the Prophet Muhammad and that of a mystic:

> Muhammad of Arabia ascended the highest Heaven and returned. 'I swear by God that if I had reached that point, I should never have returned.' These are the words of a great Muslim saint, Abdul Quddus of Gangoh. In the whole range of Sufi literature it will be probably difficult to find words which, in a single sentence, disclose such an acute perception of the psychological difference between the prophetic and the mystic types of consciousness. The mystic does not wish to return from the repose of 'unitary experience'; and even when he does return, as he must, his return does not mean much for mankind at large. The Prophet's return is creative. He returns to insert himself into the sweep of time with a view to control the forces of history, and thereby to create a fresh world of ideals. For the mystic the repose of 'unitary experience' is something final; for the Prophet it is the awakening, within him, of world-shaking psychological forces, calculated to completely transform the human world. The desire to see his religious experience transformed into a living world-force is supreme in the Prophet. Thus his return amounts to a kind of pragmatic test of the value of his religious experience. In its creative act the Prophet's will

judges both itself and the world of concrete fact in which it endeavours to objectify itself. In penetrating the impervious material before him the Prophet discovers himself for himself, and unveils himself to the eye of history.[13]

It needs to be pointed out that Iqbal himself is aware that mystic experience does not "qualitatively" differ "from the experience of the Prophet". Nor has it "now ceased to exist as a vital fact". As he continues: "Indeed the *Quran* regards both 'Anfus' (self) and 'Afaq' (world) as sources of knowledge. God reveals His signs in inner as well as outer experience, and it is the duty of man to judge the knowledge yielding capacity of all aspects of experiences. The ideal of finality, therefore, should not be taken to suggest that the ultimate fate of life is complete displacement of emotion by reason. Such a thing is neither possible nor desirable. The intellectual value of the idea is that it tends to create an independent critical attitude towards mystic experience by generating the belief that all personal authority, claiming a supernatural origin, has come to an end in the history of man. This kind of belief is a psychological force which inhibits the growth of such authority. The function of the idea is to open up fresh vistas of knowledge in the domain of man's inner experience, just as the first half of the formula of Islam has created and fostered the spirit of a critical observation of man's outer experience by divesting the forces of nature of that divine character with which earlier cultures had clothed them. Mystic experience, then, however, unusual and abnormal, must now be regarded by a Muslim as a perfectly natural experience, open to critical scrutiny like other aspects of human experience."[14]

Whatever the merit of Allama Iqbal's observations, it must, however, be borne in mind that the common denominator in both the experiences remains a fervent desire to know the Truth. Still more, the mystics' consciousness is not psychologically different from that of the Prophet. As a matter of fact, it is intrinsically the prophetic experience of ascension *(mi'raj)* that moulds mystic consciousness. It is in this sense that the most renowned Sufis of Islam always stressed the supreme importance of performing the daily prayers *(salat)* more as a means of fostering an inner link with God than merely a ritual act.

Notwithstanding the merit of Iqbal's rational analysis of the two kinds of spiritual experiences, I find it difficult to reconcile with his view that for "the mystic the repose of 'unitary experience' is something final". On the contrary, for the acknowledged leaders of the main Sufi orders, such experiences, even though incommunicable, have been the mainspring of their spiritual claim. The repository consciousness of being united in the *Tawhid-Shari'a* and *haqiqa* relationship was at the root of their endeavour to emulate the Prophet.[15] Repose is the badge of a Sufi's identity as a protege of Allah in the Quranic sense; his never-quenched desire to mould his behaviour in accordance with the prophetic role model is born not out of torpor but from his inner awakening which itself is not independent of his societal concerns. He does not deny the role of struggle in history; he seeks tranquillity of mind, spirit, and heart in shouldering the primary responsibility of carrying on the mission of the Prophet for regenerating humankind.

But for Sufis to find what I would call creative rest in their deeply-felt experience they would not have distinguished themselves both as teachers and as exemplars of the Prophet's conduct *(Sunna)*. The Sufis' consciousness, in fact, drew continued sustenance from both the 'model' and the 'ideal'. It would not, therefore, be unreasonable to assume that in their desire to imitate the 'model', the Sufis "transformed" their "religious experience" into a potent historical force. Small wonder, then, that Sufism emerged as a spiritio-social force of unrivalled universal significance in the middle ages of Islamic history.

As individual experiences of illuminated souls like those of Sufis are not communicable, so aren't the ones felt by them during the performance of daily prayers. Every believer other than the one gifted with higher spiritual consciousness, too, has moments of deep-felt religious experience, at least, once in his life. But such reasoning poses several questions: Whether an average believer is conscious of what he experiences? Whether he is able to relate his feeling or experience to the purpose of his existence? Whether he is ready to give a creative meaning to his experience for leading a purposeful life? Or then, there is a shocking question: isn't his cultivated ignorance about his spiritual potential a stumbling block in the growth of his personality as a stabilising and creative force in the cosmos?

Against the background of the foregoing discussion, it would not be difficult for us to realise that daily prayer, if performed as a means of developing an inner link with Allah rather than as a ritual, is a source of vital force and energy for one's thought and behavioural mode. A true believer's prayer is a religious experience of an indescribable nature; at the same time it may be described as both historic and subliminal affirmation of the Prophet's ascension *(mi'raj)*. For him it is not something like a routine affair but the main channel of being in direct communion with the Main Source of Energy. Doubtless, then, it is prayer which keeps the faithful on guard against recurrent dangers to which the soul is exposed in the inordinate social and economic complexities of the world.

Although according to the *Miskatu'l-Masabih,* the divine orders for prayers were originally fifty every day, the Prophet's petitionings with Allah on the eve of *mi'raj* reduced them to five. Then, when the Prophet was on his return journey to this world, he heard the message: "I have established My divine commandments, and have made them easy to My servants".[16] "Verily prayer is for the believers prescribed and timed".[17] "Seek aid with patience and prayer".[18] The importance of prayer has not only been abundantly emphasized in the *Quran,*[19] but it has been brought out in every kind of religious literature including the hagiographies of the Sufis. Apart from several benefits, including the disciplining of the soul and organising the mosque as a nucleus for orderly evolution of Muslim society, daily prayer creates a feeling of spiritual delight, elation and oneness among believers. It is not oneness of believers in merely fraternal sense but also the feeling of unity of the Creator and the created that gives *elan* to the community of believers. It is in this sense that we need to understand the profound truth underlying the Prophet's dictum that "prayer is believer's ascension". The ascent of the believer five times daily into heaven with the universal affirmation of "Allah is Great", and return to the world with the concluding prayer "The peace and mercy of Allah be with you" is both the symbolic and historic confirmation of the event of Muhammad's heavenly journey all over the universe.

The three great prophets of the Semitic religions have been Moses, Christ, and Muhammad. Being the last of the prophets and also having brought the mission of all prophets to a fruitful completion during his lifetime, Muhammad enjoys a unique position among the galaxy of prophets. Islam is not as such the youngest of all religions, as generally claimed, but the oldest. However, what gives position of unique strength to Islam in contrast to historical forms of primordial religion—Christianity and Judiasm—is its ability to renew itself in every challenging historical circumstance. In one sense, Muhammad renewed the *din-i-hanif*[20] but in another his triumphant struggle marked the perfection of primordial *din* both in religious and historical terms. But what made Islam appear as a new religion in the history of mankind was the unparalled genius of Muhammad that took both his contemporary and later detractors by surprise. Muhammad never claimed himself to be above the religion of Abraham, yet his opponents made him the butt of ridicule for founding a new religion. The greatness of Muhammad, however, lies in the fact that he was superbly able to place primordial religion on a firm spiritual and historic foundations. And it is in this sense that Islam appears young and vibrant.

Fundamentally, Islam has no quarrel with Judaism and Christianity because of their common source, i.e. Abrahamic religion. But the *Quran* is explicit on one point that Abraham was neither a Jew nor a Christian.[21] Does this mean that Abraham was a "Muhammadan"? No. The *Quran* nowhere legendizes Muhammad. The epithets used for him do not merely have supernatural connotations but carry the sense of his historic mission. Of these, the most widely used is that he was "the Grace of the Worlds".[22] This epithet assumes profound significance in the existential experience of a believer. Notwithstanding his failings in respect of conforming his conduct to the *Sunna*, a believer is not totally unmindful of his digressional behaviour. This sense of spiritual plight and anguish distinguishes the believer in the *Sunna* of Muhammad from believers in Christianity and Judaism.

The emphasis in the *Quran* that Abraham was a Muslim rather than a Christian or Jew is enough to dispel any doubt about the universality of Muhammad's role. His struggle was against distortions and aberrations of the religion that the Jews and Christians professed. The *Quran* was revealed during the course of more than twenty-two years, in the context of the Prophet's strivings, initially at the personal level, and subsequently *vis-a-vis* the challenges and problems that the Meccan society posed to him. The basic premise of the *Quran* is that the Jews and Christians had distorted the primordial religion of Abraham. One may, therefore, reasonably argue that Muhammad was not merely sent for renewing Islam but also for dispelling the mist of historical ignorance.

Ignorance is far more dangerous than any contagious disease. Still worse is the ignorance that parades as knowledge and spreads like contagion. Let us, therefore, examine the causes of this virulent disease.

In its etymological sense ignorance connotes lack of knowledge or information, unmindfulness. But in its indepth meaning ignorance denotes pride. And when learning and pride complement and supplement each other they become incestuous.

Ignorance is of several kinds. Let us begin with ignorance of the self. The state of our childhood cannot be described as an age of ignorance. The interests of childhood are the interests of humankind. Children all over the world love to play, cry and laugh in the same breath. They bring immense joy. Happiest is the atmosphere graced by the presence of children. In the East, a newly married couple's first act of sincere prayer begins with a longing for a child. God sends children not only for keeping up the progeny but also for sending ripples to our hearts and souls. And so long as we are innocent we love to remain under the loving care of our parents. But on our entry into adolescence, our knowledge of ourselves begins to grow, though in different directions.

Learning is a process; so is the evolution of human personality. The Jews, Christians and Muslims agree that Adam was the first man and the first prophet. Human knowledge began when, consequent upon error, Adam learned the first act of prayer from his Lord: "O Lord! we have wronged our own souls: If Thou forgive us not, and bestow not upon us Thy Mercy, we shall certainly be lost".[23] Adam's repentance was accepted by the Most Propitious and the Merciful. He now received the title of *Khalifat al-Allah*. And Allah said: "Descend ye from it (from the garden) altogether; and if there come unto you from Him a direction (a book and an apostle), those who follow my direction, there shall come no fear on them; nor shall they grieve in the world to come; for they shall enter paradise; but they who disbelieve and accuse our signs of falsehood, these shall be companions of the fire; they shall remain therein for ever."[24]

Falsehood is repugnant to Truth. This is what all prophets have preached. If human knowledge rests on truth, how does error then masquerade as knowledge? Error does not spring as much from ignorance as from presumptuousness. But being too bold and self-confident without the necessary authority is a sign of pride rather than discretion. According to the philosopher John Locke, "Error is not a fault of our knowledge, but a mistake of our judgement giving assent to that which is not true." And as Horace Walpole remarks: "In all science error precedes the truth and it is better it should go first than last." Errors occur because there is some charm hidden in them. Contrary to darkness with which ignorance is generally equated, an error has a glimmer of light through the mist of ignorance. This phenomenon may be described as the refraction of eternal light lying down below the horizon.

All prophets were in search of that Light. Abraham's case makes the point abundantly clear. According to the *Quran*, his search for the Light began with inquisitiveness. He questioned the contemporary practice of worshipping images or idols as deities. But in his quest for knowledge he took the star, the moon and the sun for his Lord in chain succession. Since the lordship of heavenly bodies changed in rotation, the momentary ideal of adoring them could not continue. Having realised the error of his judgement in following false light, Abraham ultimately affirmed: "Verily I direct my face towards Him who hath created the heavens and the earth, following the right religion, and I am not of the polytheists."[25]

The heritage that Abraham bequeathed has formed a fundamental part of Muslim worship and ethos. In terms of history he struggled against deification of images and natural objects. As a prophet of the Gospel of Unity, the sheet-anchor of eternal spiritual Truth, the *Quran* describes him as a model and an *imam*.[26] He was the first prophet who launched a struggle in history in both spiritual and social terms. He founded the Ka'ba, the House of Allah, as a unique symbol of the Unity of the Lord of the Worlds. "Remember He made the House a place of assembly for men and a place of safety; and take ye the station of Abraham as a place of prayer; and We covenanted with Abraham and Isma'il, that they should sanctify My House for who compass it round, or use it as a retreat, or bow, or prostrate themselves (therein in prayer)."[27] Again: "And remember Ibrahim and Isma'il raised the foundations of the House (with this prayer): 'Our Lord accept (This service) from us: for Thou art the All-Hearing, the All-Knowing; Our Lord make of us Muslims, bowing to Thy (will), and of our progeny a people Muslim bowing to Thy (will); and show us our places for the celebration of (due) rites; and turn unto us (in Mercy); for Thou art the Oft-Relenting Most Merciful. Our Lord send amongst them a Messenger of their own who shall rehearse Thy Signs to them and instruct them in Scripture and wisdom, and purify them; for Thou art the Exalted in Might, The Wise."[28]

The history of Muslims is not in conflict with the *Quran*. The Ka'ba stands not only on the pedestal of the great Truth but also on history. Never in history have Muslims ever felt the need for raising another Ka'ba. Instead, their homes, open fields or enclosed gardens, offices or public places and above all mosques are places of prostration towards Ka'ba. History bears an elaborate testimony to the fact that there does not exist more than one house of Allah on the earth for believers who surrendered to the will of Allah. Facing Ka'ba in each prayer does not signify facing Mecca as is generally understood. It signifies cleansing of the soul of all idols and worldly ideologies. Didn't Muhammad purify the Ka'ba of the tribal idols it housed on the eve of his triumphant march into Mecca? Didn't he restore the universal character of the Ka'ba as the prostrating place of the one true God? It is not the daily prayer alone, but, also, the annual pilgrimage *(Hajj)* that underscores the affirmation of faith in the unity of one God. As the pilgrims from all parts of the globe approach Mecca they shout, "I am here, O Lord, I am here". The surrender to Allah does not amount to obliteration but exaltation of the human personality to the loftiest heights against patriarchal and hegemonistic worldviews.

A benediction recited in the daily prayers is also traditionally believed to exalt believers in one God. Not only by virtue of its blessings, but also in view of the fact that it clearly describes Muhammad's role in history as renewer of primordial religion of Abraham, it is worthy to quote: "O God, have mercy on Muhammad and his descendants, as Thou didst have mercy on Ibrahim and on his descendants. Thou art to be praised, and Thou art great. O God, bless Muhammad and his descendants as Thou didst bless Ibrahim and his descendants. Thou art to be praised and Thou art great." This imploring for mercy provides a connecting link between all descendants of Abraham. What is more, Muhammad, while reviving the *Sunna* of Abraham, brought out a remarkable synthesis of the *Sunna* of all prophets in his model behaviour. Since the *Sunna* of Muhammad gained precedence because of its uniquely synthetic, spiritual and historical character over that of all other prophets, Muhammad became a perfect model for humanity.

Among various rituals associated with the pilgrimage to Mecca, a visit to the Plain of Arafat deserves special mention. Here the pilgrims, from noon to sunset, stand before Allah in open repentance, seeking His pardon for themselves and all Muslims throughout the world. Here is a hill called the Mount of Mercy from which the Prophet delivered his last sermon or message during his Farewell Pilgrimage. Muhammad's call—"O people, verily your Lord is one and your father is one. All of you belong to Adam and Adam was made of clay. There is no superiority for an Arab over a non-Arab nor for a non-Arab over an Arab; nor for a white-coloured over a black-coloured; nor for a black-skinned and a white-skinned except in piety. Verily the noblest among you is he who is the most pious"—has relevance for all times which is why it is repeated every year by the preacher before a gathering of a Muslim community across the world that transcends national, racial, economic, and sexual barriers.

Muslims, throughout the day during prayer, and on the eve of pilgrimage, reaffirm their faith in the Oneness of Allah and the finality of the prophethood of Muhammad. While the uncompromising monotheistic idea of oneness or unity *(tawhid)* of God cuts at the root of polytheism, the affirmation of belief in Muhammad as the last and final prophet of humanity raises Islam high above ethnocentrism. Muhammad is not the Prophet of a particular group or community of believers but the Prophet of mankind. Moulding ourselves into a community of believers does not mean adoration of Muhammad but demands the praxis orientation of our soul, thought and social behaviour in consonance with the Quranic and historic dimensions of his human personality.

Notes and References

1. *Quran,* 10/47; 16/36.
2. Ibid., 33/40.
3. Ibid., 94/4.
4. Ibid., 10/37-38.
5. According to Allama Yusuf Ali, "The Mother of the Book, the Foundation of Revelation, the Preserved Tablet *(Lauh Mahfuz)* (85/22), is the core or essence of revelation, the original principle or fountainhead of Allah's Eternal and Universal Law. From this fountainhead are derived all streams of knowledge and wisdom, that flow through time and feed the intelligence of created minds. The Mother of the Book is in Allah's own Presence, and its dignity and wisdom are more than all we can think of." See *Holy Quran,* trans., Allama Yusuf Ali, n. 4606.
6. The *Quran* says that men do not perceive *(la yash'urun).*
7. "Will they not then ponder on the *Quran (afala yata dabbarun al-Quran)?* If it had been from other than Allah they would have found therein much incongruity." (Ibid., 4/82).
8. The *Quran* repeatedly states that righteous are those who reflect on its verses in addition to pondering the creation of the heavens and the earth and affirm: "Our Lord, you have not created this creation in vain" ibid., 3/191; 21/16, etc.
9. The cardinal argument of the *Quran* is that men are gifted with the faculties of reason and perception. Yet most of them are sunk in utter darkness. "So they could not see. Deaf, dumb and blind, they will not return (to the path)." Ibid., 2/17-18. At another place: "Many are the jinns and men We have made for Hell: They have hearts wherewith they understand not, eyes wherewith they see not, and ears wherewith they hear not. They are like cattle—nay more misguided: for they are heedless (of warning)". Ibid., 7/179.
10. "O mankind! Verily there hath come to you a convincing proof from your Lord for We have sent unto you a light (that is) manifest." Ibid., 4/174. And Allama Yusuf Ali rightly observes: "The Proof and the Light are the *Quran* and the Personality, Life, and Teachings of Muhammad Al-Mustafa". op. cit., 679 n.
11. Doing everything as beautifully as possible, called *ihsan,* implies perfection in spiritual terms which consists also in worshipping God "as if you were seeing Him, for if you do not see Him, He sees you."
12. For a detailed discussion on the concept of *wahat al-wujud* and *wahdat al-shuhud,* see Ishaq Khan, "Sufism in Indian History", *Muslim Shrines in India,* ed. Christian W. Troll (Oxford, 1989), pp. 275-291; also *idem, Kashmir's Transition to Islam: The Role of Muslim Rishis* (Manohar, New Delhi, 1994), pp. 115-16 and note 27.

13. Mohammad Iqbal, *The Reconstruction of Religious Thought in Islam,* Kitab Bhavan (New Delhi, 1981), p.124.
14. Ibid., p. 127.
15. See Ishaq Khan, *Kashmir's Transition to Islam,* p. 120.
16. Originally compiled by Imam Husain al-Baghawi (d. A.H. 510 or 516), the reputed commentator, who called it *Masabihus-Sunnah* or the "Lamps of the Traditions." This well-known work, dealing with Sunni tradition, was revised by Shaikh Waliyu'd-Din in A.H. 737 who besides adding an additional chapter to each section named it *Mishkatu'l Masabih* or the "Niche of Lamps". Abdul Haqq Muhaddis of Delhi translated the work into Persian during the reign of emperor Akbar, and added a commentary.
17. *Quran,* 4/1-4.
18. Ibid., 2/42
19. Ibid., 1/1-7, 2/110; 4/101-1-4; 13/14-15; See also 2/238-239; 3/8; 26-27, 147, 191-194; 4/43, 5/6, 11/114; 17/78-81; 23/118; 50/29-40; 52/48-49; 73/1-8, 203.
20. Abraham was sincere and firm in faith. Hence the religion of Abraham was the one that was true and existed from the beginning of the cosmos. The pristine purity of his natural religion was based on unshakeable faith in the One True God. "They say: 'Become Jews or Christians if ye would be guided to (salvation).' say thou: 'Nay'. (I would rather the Religion of Abraham the True *(millat-i-Ibrahima hanifa)*, and he joined not gods with Allah." Ibid., 2/135.
21. *Quran,* 3/67. Abraham was not a pagan. Ibid., 3/95. "....But he, (Abraham) was upright *(hanifa)*, and bowed his will to Allah's (which is Islam) and he joined no gods with Allah." Ibid., 3/67.
22. Ibid., 21/107.
23. Ibid., 7/23.
24. Ibid., 2/38-39.
25. Ibid., 6/79.
26. Ibid., 16/120.
27. Ibid., 2/125.
28. Ibid., 2/127-129.

4

MUHAMMAD AND SPIRITUAL ETHICS

The degeneracy of man in modern civilisation has perhaps sunk to its lowest depths notwithstanding his accomplishments in all the sciences. Modern man freely and proudly calls himself democratic, secular, socialist, liberal, and above all, an adherent of "religious ideology". In fact, we are fond of using such epithets for ourselves in accordance with our beliefs in systems or ideologies. We are more or less addicted to our ideologies mainly for the sake of proving ourselves right and others wrong, no matter if it amounts to pernicious influence on society. Our proclivity to demonstrate the strength of our convictions by acrimonious debate rather than practice has been at the root of conflicts. True, a thorough discussion on issues concerning our beliefs and ideologies has served the cause of human knowledge, but it has rarely promoted our understanding of ourselves. And but for the lack of such an understanding there would have been no continued bloodshed in the name of political and religious ideologies.

Our lack of understanding of ourselves may be attributed to the glitter and grandeur of modern civilisation which has impaired the inner reasoning of our mind and soul. Simultaneously, it is no less attributable to the complexity of our nature as humans, and to the varied structures of both the individual and collective psyche of our mind. The modern man's chief preoccupation has been the material world. And even those who claim to be struggling against secular and materialistic ideologies for serving the cause of Islam, or for that matter, other religions, have actually been instrumental in pushing the spiritual world to the walls. The greatest weapon in the hands of an adherent of a religious cause should have been the inner strength of his soul and mind. Unfortunately, however, spiritual or moral force is being replaced by brute force in every aspect of our life. With the growing race for arms, humanity's attention has turned from pursuing higher goals to the publicly weak and childish aspect of exhibiting the strength of scientific achievement in vulgar forms of protest.

Example is profoundly better than precept. The absolute epitome of both precept and example was the Prophet Muhammad. There is no doubt about his being a paragon of all human virtues. He did not construct abstractions but all through his life evolved the perfect model of personality in his human sociality. Muhammad was born in an environment which had given him an aptitude for serious thinking and contemplation. The social environment was the most favourable for the optimum development of his human personality. How could he suppress the inner struggle, effort, and suffering from his spiritual manhood? Wasn't he sent to the world for preventing the degeneracy of man in every hopeless situation?

Muhammad was unlettered *(ummi)*. But this fact did not prove a stumbling block in the flowering of his personality. The inner reasoning of his soul and mind, however, proved itself to be more powerful in moulding his supernal personality rather than merely any supernatural factor itself. Muhammad's greatest merit was his ability to comprehend life in the depths of his growing consciousness. His early life was not shrouded in mystery but was a flowering of tender and complex realities.

Muhammad was the posthumous son of a trader, Abd Allah, who belonged to the family of Hashim, the noblest tribe of Quraish, tracing their descent from Isma'il. His father and the grandfather of Muhammad, Abd al-Mutalib, held the exalted office of the custodian of the Ka'ba. Born in A.D. 570 his mother, Amina died when he was only six years old. Abu Talib, Muhammad's uncle, took loving care of his nephew. Muhammad's occupation, as a young boy, was to tend the sheep and goats of Mecca upon the neighbouring hills and valleys. Later, he joined the service of Khadija, a rich widow of Mecca, as a steward or business manager for her caravans. This was the period which coincided with the emergence of Central Arabia as a major commercial power. While Mecca was at the crossroads between the Indian Ocean and the Mediterranean, it also lay astride important trade routes that extended from Africa across the Middle East to China and Malaysia. As the leader of Khadija's merchandise, Muhammad travelled the same route which he had traversed in the company of his uncle thirteen years before. His journeys to Busra, Aleppo and Damascus must have brought him in contact with both Jews and Christians. Although apparently committed to the worship of one God, they were at loggerheads with one another. This fact together with the idolatry and social atrophy of Meccans must have made Muhammad reflective.

Muhammad discharged his commercial duties in such a conscientious manner that Khadija was highly impressed. This led to their marriage. Here is a point of reflection for us. In the ordinary sense, marriage has a biological basis, and generally a young man desires to marry a girl younger than him in age. But how is it that Muhammad, a young boy of 25 years, married a widow of 40 years? Was he lured by the riches of Khadija? Not at all, as evidence negates the very idea of posing a question of that sort. Muhammad's marriage with Khadija was not marriage in the ordinary sense, but a union of two souls in close spiritual and social interaction. The nobility and piety of this spiritual bond lay in the ties of perfect friendship, confidence, faithfulness and understanding. The perpetual friendship between the two would not have been possible without the confidence of both in each other's integrity. Connubial happiness resulted in two sons and four daughters. While Muhammad's happy married life kept the moral world in being, it saved man from sinking into licentiousness. Both he and Khadija provided a kind of discipline in domestic education, refinement and mutual understanding worthy of emulation. Tradition tells us that the marriage of the orphaned Muhammad and Khadija was solemnised by the wholesale distribution of the rich lady's wealth among the poor. The story that the newly married couple's home did not have even oil for lighting the lamp is symbolic of Khadija's faithfulness to Muhammad who, in spite of his enterprising skills in business affairs, was not materialistic.

Before marriage, Muhammad had successfully and honestly organised a commercial enterprise of Khadija, but after marriage he preferred to live a life of chosen poverty. There can be no better example than this in human history of reciprocal satisfaction derived in poverty while remaining in the conjugal state for so many years. Their marriage has more of beauty and seriousness and lessons for men in search of truth. Their honeymoon was not an act of senseless revelry but it was revelatory of their concern for suffering humanity. Even in affluence they had learnt the necessary relations of the cosmic universe, of their fellowmen, of their inner selves, and also those of their heart and mind. There is a clearness and accuracy of thought for the thoughtful in Muhammad's marriage with Khadija. A certain relationship between the two, susceptible of being described mathematically, is revealed in yet another aspect of their married life.

Muhammad had made his mark as a respectable gentleman in a society in "which traditional tribal ways were strained by Mecca's transition from a semi-Bedouin to a commercial, urban society".[1] But so rampant were the moral ills of this thriving commercial centre that a model of a completely developed man had become a rarity. Muhammad's impeccable moral conduct and sobriety of judgement did not go unnoticed among the citizens of Mecca who, out of love and respect, popularly called him *al-Amin*, "The Trustworthy". One of Muhammad's serious engagements was to retreat regularly to a cave on Mt. Hira, a few miles north of Mecca. Here he contemplated and reflected in solitude on the idolatry, moral degeneration, and factious rivalries of his people. Here at the age of forty during a night of Ramadan, called "The Night of Power and Excellence" (*Lailat al-Qadar* or *Shab-i-Qadr*), he first received the divine answer to the yearning of his soul and mind. "Recite", commanded the angel Gabriel. Muhammad responded in bewilderment that he was 'unlettered'. The heavenly intermediary insisted twice more, and each time the 'unlettered' seeker after the Truth expressed his inability to read. Then Light dawned upon Muhammad, and the words of Allah came to him:

> Read in the name of your Lord who created. He created man out of a germ-cell. Read for your Lord is the Most Beneficent. One who has taught the use of the pen, taught man that which he did not know.[2]

Muhammad repeated the words with a frightened heart. Returning home from the cave, he asked Khadija: "Wrap me up, wrap me up". And he was wrapped up in a garment; until his fear vanished, he told his wife about the experience at the cave. Fearing that he was possessed, Khadija, who had intimately known her husband, responded to Muhammd's remark— "I was afraid I should die"—in these words: "No, it will not be so, I swear by God, He will never make thee melancholy or sad. For you are kind to your relatives, you speak the truth, you are faithful in trust, you bear the afflictions of the people, you spend in good works what you gain in trade, you are hospitable, and you assist your fellowmen."

Khadija then took her husband to her Christian cousin, Waraqa ibn Naufal. When the Christian sage heard of Muhammad's experience, the reassurance poured forth: "Surely, by Him in whose hand is Waraqa's soul, thou art the prophet of this people. There hath come unto thee the greatest Namus (the Archangel Gabriel) who came unto Moses. Like the Hebrew prophets, Thou wilt be called a liar, and they will use thee despitefully and cast thee out and fight against thee."[3]

Thereupon Muhammad believed himself to be the Prophet and addressed himself to the noblest mission of educating the people sunk in utter darkness and ignorance. He continued to receive revelations and his message won him a few converts. And what is of significance to emphasize is that the first convert to Islam was the woman, his faithful wife Khadija. What greater happiness was there for two human souls than to feel that they were joined not only for conjugal but also for spiritual life. When the Meccan people called the *al-Amin* an impostor and a cheat, Khadija stood by the Prophet. The recognition of Muhammad as the "Apostle of God" by a woman is no less revelatory. At least, the recognition of Muhammad's spiritual manhood by Khadija elevates Muslim women to a higher dignity in life—above and beyond the begetting of children.

Had Muhammad been celibate, he would not have been the most perfect model of human personality. Nor would his spiritual experience been a perfect experience in human terms had he not shared it with his partner. Wasn't his home the first seminary of precept and example? Wasn't his family circle the supreme conductor of primordial religion that he was destined to bring to fruition? The cardinal element in Muhammad's home environment was love and confidence which increased with the years. Muhammad, like Christian mystics before him, would not have returned home after experiencing the spiritual experience had not his mind and soul something healthy and fruitful to reflect upon while living in wedded bliss.

The house of Muhammad was marked by its serenity, brightness and happiness in the midst of darkness and ignorance that characterised almost every household in an iniquitous social order. The Prophet's conjugal life with his first wife thus proved to be not a contract of convenience but a solemn contract of spiritual understanding. It was the solid bond of true love for uprooting falsehood in order to build up both the human personality and homely atmosphere in the unhomely world within the limits of spiritual ethics of the *Quran*. The history of the reaffirmation of faith in the Will of Allah was thus consummated in the married life of Muhammad and Khadija. The story of this life was not romantic but realistic; it was not woven around fables but based on shared sacrifices of matrimonial unity with readiness and cheerfulness. Martin Luther, the German religious reformer, is worthy of quote here: "God has set the type of marriage everywhere throughout the creation. Every creature seeks its perfection in another. The very heavens and earth picture it to us". Didn't Muhammad's marriage with Khadija at the age of 25 and the recognition of his supernal human personality fifteen years later by his elderly wife secure the domestic world from an untimely dissolution? Didn't this marriage rest on the bedrock of love and charity? The greatest Kashmiri troubadour of mystical love, Shaikh Nuruddin Rishi (1379-1442), draws a clear distinction between the life of a recluse and that of a dutiful householder on the basis of his own experiences. Thus, after spending twelve years in a cave, the Shaikh realised that physical seclusion associated with asceticism, however useful it may be in the inculcation of self-discipline, does not make up its essence. Rather, it lies in emulating the example of the Prophet Muhammad:

> There are jackals and monkeys in the forests
> The caves are infested with rats;
> Those who offer prayers five times a day to
>   wash off the dirt of their heart;
> Those who lead a family life, they are privileged
> A dutiful householder will be crowned (with success on the
>   Day of Judgment);
> The messenger of Allah (Muhammad) led a marital life and
>   won the Divine grace.[4]

The first ten years of Muhammad's mission in the cause of Islam were troublesome, "marked by Meccan rejection and resistance."[5] Their hostility was aroused mainly on account of his denunciation of the tribal idols that the Ka'ba housed. The monotheism preached by the *Quran* was uncompromising.[6] It cut at the very root of the dignity and authority that the tribal leaders of Mecca enjoyed as keepers of the Ka'ba.[7] The Quranic emphasis on the Oneness of Allah and equality of believers professed to His transcendental Unity transcended ethnocentrism of the Meccans based on tribal bonds. Furthermore, the *Quran's* disapprobation of socio-economic inequalities of Meccan life,[8] moral atrophy, false contracts, usury[9], and the neglect and exploitation of orphans[10], women [11] and the poor[12] was ominous for the political and economic privileges, authority and prestige they enjoyed as keepers of the central sanctuary of Arabian tribal religion. Also, Muhammad's claim to prophethood and his insistence that all true believers belonged to a single universal community *(umma)* had serious implications for undermining the solidarity of Meccan political authority based on tribal ethnocentric beliefs.

The outstanding trait of Muhammad's personality was his insistence both on being the servant *(abd)* and messenger *(rasul)* of Allah. Raising the first finger of the right hand during each prayer *(salat)* synchronises with a believer's recitation that "I testify that there is no deity but God; and I testify that Muhammad is the servant of God, and the messenger of God". This practice is the foundation of the Islamic faith. Although recital of the word *(kalima)* "There is no deity but God: Muhammad is the Apostle of God" is undisputedly the first of the five foundations or pillars of Islam, its recital with insertion "Muhammad is the servant of God" by the Prophet himself formed the basic percept for serving humanity. True, in the *Quran* Muhammad is also addressed as His servant, but its repeated recital in daily prayer elevates the personality of the Prophet to the greatest heights. The belief in the Oneness of Allah, Prophethood of Muhammad and his servantship of Allah *(ubudiyyat)* awakens in a believer the consciousness of his importance as an individual. And without doubt the preaching of Muhammad opened a momentous chapter in the history of human struggle against tyranny and exploitation of every kind. It was the struggle for the recognition of the selfhood of suppressed and deprived individuals and a vindication of their rights in an oppressive world order. But it must be pointed out that in this struggle the Prophet stood forth as the champion of the weak against the strong, though even in the pre-Islamic class-conscious society his social position was by all accounts pre-eminent.

With the birth of elementary consciousness, an individual begins to feel himself in various fetters. The first act towards gaining freedom from the shackles of this world begins with a child's defiance of his parents commands, however small it may look to an unimaginative mind. But as his consciousness nourishes and grows as a result of good upbringing, his personality moulds into that of a sophisticated gentleman. Children born in poor families have rare or very little opportunities for developing into attractive personalities. However, in spite of the yawning gulf existing between the rich and the poor, they share a common personality trait. This relates to the commonality of their belief and thinking obsessed with the petty concerns of the mundane world. The social basis of the relationship between the haves and have-nots is rooted in this obsessional worldliness. No wonder, then, that the haughtiness of being rich and a sense of deprivation, characterising social consciousness, germinates hatred and violence in the world. Class consciousness and prejudices have not only been at the very root of almost all troubles in this world but also the sole cause of the destruction of human souls.

Muhammad's mission was to free mankind from the chains of ignorance, soullessness, ethnocentrism, and above all, from the tyranny of the class-conscious mind. Negative impulses such as pride, hatred, jealousy, etc., stem mostly from the soullessness and ethnocentric thoughtfulness of a particular social order. It is a truism to say that social problems exist in any given society; hence, the ingrained pessimism of certain individuals leads them to think that their efforts can hardly put an end to the ills of their society. Muhammad's historic role, however, belies such morbid thinking with its relegation of individuals to passive roles in the *status quo*.

If historical events were merely due to the conflicts of social forces caused by man's material needs and political ambitions, what was the need for never-ceasing struggle of human souls for evolving spiritual ethics *vis-a-vis* the deep-felt malaise of their societies? Such consciousness has characterised the inner struggle of sensitive souls in various societies. However, it must be remembered that, in contrast to Islam, non-Muslim societies could not develop the viability of their spiritual ethics on universal norms. In spite of the monotheistic conceptions of God in Judaism and Christianity, neither of these historical religions have ever brought home the ideal of the One God of humanity in such clear terms as did Islam in the religious behaviour of its adherents. The repeated emphasis of Muhammad on the fundamental tenets of Islam—recitation of the creed, daily prayer, fasting, alms and annual pilgrimage—point to the eternal need for galvanisation of human effort in the direction of attaining spiritual and social stability on this planet on universalist rather than ethnocentric norms. Not only are the fundamental Islamic rituals oriented to the longing of individual souls, but they are marked by an abiding merit of generating both inner and social consciousness of being a citizen of this world and the Hereafter. The rights of a believer's citizenship are not confined to a particular society or country, but in the Quranic sense, he has the right to inherit the world[13] without remaining wedded to it in any ideological way. In another sense every believer as a *Khalifa* can inherit the world by working among men anywhere, and make his divine commission felt in the heart, soul and mind of inquisitive seekers anywhere in the globe. The importance attached to travels by Sufis needs to be understood in this context also.

The yearnings of Muḥammad's soul and his individual role in Arab society in response to divine command gave birth to a new academic discipline which we call Spiritual Ethics. The science of this discipline developed during a period of over 22 years following Muhammad's experience at the cave of Hira. During this period the Prophet, notwithstanding his exalted status, was commissioned to create a model of personality in the face of trials and tribulations. The task was Herculean given the magnitude of the challenges to which he was exposed. But ultimately he emerged successful against serious odds through concerted efforts of the soul and mind towards the fruition of the deeply cherished goal of stabilising the inner and outer world of believers in one God. The Prophet's struggle had three essential components, namely, yearning, guidance and teaching.

History tells us that no great achievement in the world has been possible without an ambition or desire. However, every noble goal had its birth in solitude. Muhammad did not think in the midst of commercial development of his society, but far from the ugly and insolent riches of the maddening crowd. He did not want to live the life of the herd but was accustomed to living in comparative and contemplative recesses of his inner soul. Although intimacy and sociability were the distinctive traits of the Prophet's personality, yet even in the company of men quiet moments were not exceptional in his existence. Since the Prophet longed for the contemplation of truth, establishment of peace within was the prime requisite for attaining the noble goal. In order to understand spiritual consciousness, it is therefore necessary to realise that spiritual activity is essentially an entirely personal undertaking. It is a kind of thirst for higher knowledge in all its external totality, and surely it brings to man the fulfilment of his highest desire: invigorating spirit, light, divine love, ineffable peace. Wasn't the Quranic revelation also the fruit of Muhammad's longing for such knowledge?

The *Quran* was intrinsically sent as a Book of Guidance for mankind. In the strict terms of the *Quran* the Real Guide *(Hadi)*[14] of humankind is Allah. Muhammad is a "messenger",[15] "warner"[16] and harbinger of "glad tidings"[17]. But then he is a teacher as well. As the Divine Book of Guidance, the *Quran* is primarily addressed to the man as an individual and then as a member of society.

Every individual has a history unlike all others; and each society has a history different from the rest. Each individual is unique in himself. As Alexis Carrel, the French scientist and the Nobel laureate, observes: "Everyone is defined simultaneously by the number, quality and intensity of his psychological activities. There are no individuals of identical mentality. Indeed, those whose consciousness is rudimentary closely resembles each other. The richer the personality, the greater the individual difference. All the activities of consciousness rarely develop at the same time in one individual. There is a marked difference not only in the intensity of those functions, but also in their quality. Moreover, the number of their possible combinations is infinite. No task is more difficult than to analyse the constitution of a given individual".[18]

Although accurate classification of individuals is beyond mental reach or psychological analysis, yet psychoanalysts categorise certain individuals according to their intellectual, affective, moral, aesthetic, religious or mystical characteristics. However, the study of psychological individuality of certain personalities like hysteric, megalomanic, neurotic, demented, pessimistic, optimistic, moralistic, aesthetic, intellectual, snobbish, etc., is possible—even though considering the uniqueness of each type—it may be deceptive to a certain degree. Small wonder that the individuality of spiritually or divinely elevated personality is beyond any psychoanalysis. Spirituality and its infinite potentialities are not measurable. But it is significant that years after the death of the Prophet when Aisha, the youngest wife of Muhammad, was asked about the moral behaviour of her illustrious husband, she unhesitatingly remarked that the Prophet himself was the *Quran* personified.

The sociology of spiritual ethics is the knowledge of ourselves gained through precept and its practice in daily life. Knowledge is worse than ignorance if not transmitted, felt, expounded, explored, and above all, practised. The very fact that the Prophet was first asked to "read" rather than rule epitomises his role as the greatest teacher of humankind. The Prophet's greatness is embedded in the very dynamic of his supernal and historical personality. The dimensional depths of his supernal and historical personality were infinite. He was set a task very different from that of other great men of history. He did not come to this world to found an ideological system but rather to redeem the personality of individuals. As a perfect teacher, he took into account the nature of man, his unity, as well as uniqueness. The higher aim was to relieve the suffering of the individual and to cure him. He did not use magic or medicine but the natural purity of his precept and practice to cure the afflicted souls. He, therefore, differed profoundly from other teachers. The noblest task of imparting knowledge to humanity was not knowledge as commonly understood or as preserved in the libraries but it was a continuous process of interaction between the human soul and human society. Knowledge for the Prophet was a rigorous discipline of the soul and behaviour than merely of thought. He did not specialise in any particular branch of knowledge in the modern sense but ceaselessly practised and actualised the concrete truths of the universal knowledge contained in the *Quran*, in the exemplified human and moral excellence of his social behaviour. That he was an absolute epitome of a universal teacher was remarkably testified to in Islamic history by all Sufis of the main orders who considered themselves to be mere seekers of knowledge personified by the Prophet. In order to understand in depth the impact of the Prophet's personality on his contemporaries, we may return to the theme of conversion.

We have seen that Khadija's submission to Islam was more than conversion in any sense. As a matter of fact, her soul and mind had begun experiencing spiritual transmutation while seeing the scrupulous manner in which her business affairs were managed by the young man of perfect moral excellence and impeccable integrity. Further, the happiness of her conjugal life bore the deep impress of her husband's kindness to relatives, truthfulness, faithfulness in trust, compassion, generosity, humour, philanthrophy, hospitality and fellowship. It is no surprise, therefore, that in the history of the Quranic revelation the Truth was recognised remarkably by the delicacy of a woman's sensibility. For Khadija, the Truth was not a dogma but a practical activity of the human personality which was simultaneously a means of creative communication. The revolutionary remaking of the old and the building of the new society was only possible given the ability of the Prophet to practise, define, teach and verify the Truth. Since the Prophet was the embodiment of moral good and virtue, his personality was the only criterion of what is moral. As evil and amorality in the Meccan society were at their peak, the moral authority of the Prophet was by no means invulnerable. The genius of the Prophet was his perspicacity that no moral code, even if divine, could be imposed from above. The historical form of the Quranic morality was the Prophet's social behaviour *(Sunna)* which included its basic universal moral norms and elaborated by his moral struggle against the social yoke and prevalent immorality during a period of over 22 years.

The peaceful transition of Meccan society from moral atrophy to moral rejuvenation was more than a revolution in the history of morality of the whole humanity. The Prophet's morality provided the model and the highest standard of conduct to which his contemporaries were an eyewitness. Such a standard of morality was not merely confined to his behaviour, but it naturally proved to be a vital force in bringing about sublime transformation of his society. The moral norms of Islam were, then, sanctioned not by the Meccan political authority but by the force of diffusion and public opinion; and their evolution and formation took root in the moral consciousness of the Arab society spontaneously and not merely as a result of divinely promulgated law. The question of the application of the norms of the *Quran* was intrinsically a matter of attitudes. In this sense, the history of Islam, in response to the Prophet Muhammad's message, was also a matter of attitudes. It is this story of transition from certain, historically limited, ingrained habits of mind to universal moral consciousness that the following chapter has to relate.

Notes and References

1. John L. Eposito, *Islam: The Straight Path*, Oxford University Press, New York, 1988, p.8.
2. *Quran*, 96/1
3. Guillaume, A. trans. *The Life of Muhammad*, Oxford University Press, London, 1955, p.107.
4. Ishaq Khan, *Kashmir's Transition to Islam*, p.133.
5. Eposito, op. cit., p.10.
6. *Quran*, 107/1-6; 104/1-6.
7. Ibid., 65/11; 104/1-9; 113/1-5; 141/1-6.
8. Ibid., 5/1. See Allama Yusuf Ali, trans. *The Holy Quran*, 682 n; also Appendix No.7.
9. Ibid., 3/130.
10. Ibid., 4/10; 107/1-2, etc.
11. The fourth *sura* of the Quran is named *"The Woman" (Al Nisa)* and describes their rights in respect of marriage, property and inheritance.
12. Ibid., 107/1-7.
13. See Ibid., 21/105; 28/5; 7/128, 137; 39/74; 44/28. It must be borne in mind that material gifts of the world in terms of wealth, property and government are not more than trust; they finally revert to Allah. "To Allah belongs the heritage of the heavens and the earth..." Ibid., 3/180. While Allah makes the pious inherit the world in the sense of *amana*, inheritance in spiritio-historical perspective is a warning and a lesson for those who covet worldly glory without the thought of the Hereafter: "How many were the gardens and springs they left behind, and cornfields and noble buildings, and pleasant things

wherein they had taken such delight! Thus (was their end)! And We
made other people inherit (those things)! And neither heaven nor
earth shed a tear over them: nor were they given a respite (again)".
Ibid., 44/25-29.

14. "...Say: Allah's guidance is the (only) guidance, and we have been
directed to submit ourselves to the Lord of the Worlds". Ibid., 6/71,
88; 92/12 etc.

15. "Muhammad is no more than a messenger..." Ibid., 3/144. "We
have sent thee but as a (messenger) to all mankind, giving them glad
tidings, and warning them (against sin), but most men know not."
Ibid., 53/56-62; 34/28.

16. Ibid., 7/184, 188; 15/89.

17. Ibid., 34/28, etc.

18. Alexis Carrel, *Man the Unknown*, Penguin, New York, 1948, pp. 224-
225.

5

ATTITUDES AND APPROACHES
TO ISLAM

The Islamic ideal is the highest standard of perfection or
excellence and hence the ultimate objective or aim of a believer
who has an imagination or a conception of something in its
perfection. For the contemporaries of the Prophet Muhammad
the ideal did not exist merely in their imagination but in objective
historical reality. The Prophet did not exist independently of
them nor did they of his radiant personality. Contrary to this, the
position of the modern man is radically different. He is separated
from the Prophetic model by a very long distance of over 14
centuries. In either case, however, habits of mind and action that
one displays over a length of time in imitation of the model are
worthy of note. The prevailing aspect of one's mind is shown in
one's behaviour and in relationship with others. Attitudes thus
emerge as a result of certain habits of mind in relationship with
social reality. Attitudes may be assumed for imitative effect or
vice versa. In both forms of attitudes, the interplay of mental,
volitional and emotional elements is evident.

So long as Muhammad did not claim himself to be the
Prophet, the attitude of the Meccans towards him was deeply
respectful. In spite of his young age, the warring tribes of Mecca
sought his advice and accepted his judgement in the settlement of
their disputes. Not only did they repose trust and confidence in
the Prophet, but his pleasing manners, charitable acts,
compassion and love for children had endeared him to the
Meccans notwithstanding their moral turpitude. But the moment
Muhammad proclaimed the unity of oneness of God in defiance
of polytheism of Meccan society, attitudes began to take several
forms at the individual and social levels.

Arab society was fragmented before the advent of Muhammad as the Prophet. The ethnocentrism of the tribal Arabs was a partly conscious but largely unconscious tendency. The tribal consciousness of being one was not more than loyalty to one's own group. This kind of consciousness had perpetuated and ensured the evil of slavery to such an extent that consequent degradation of man had turned the slave-master into a brute and slave into the most despicable of creatures on earth. Slavery in its all forms and in all its magnitude had ruptured the sacred ties of souls and hurt best affections. With the result that while the mind of the slave had become slavish, or in other words, degraded, that of the master was atrociously and outrageously debased.

Within the narrow limits of ethnocentric society, the human personality was hardly capable of recognising itself. Both the slave and his master's personalities were only self-conscious to the degree of their respective roles in the society. Their attitudes were, therefore, the result of what I have already described as a partly conscious but largely unconscious proclivity. Given the mechanism of the slave-owning system, consciousness and behaviour of the master and the slave were conditioned. It would be presumptuous to aver that there was an undercurrent of hostility in the consciousness of the slave against his master. As an institution, slavery survived even after the advent of Islam. Although social antagonism in the modern sense did not exist in the slave-owning system, yet Islam played a significant role in bringing about a radical transformation in the attitude of masters towards slaves. Given the stage of historical development of the tribal society, the slaves were not below the threshold of consciousness regarding their social position. This is the reason that after their entry into Islam they did not fail to promote the spirit of egalitarianism in the consciousness of Muslims to the highest degree.

The *Quran* urged the just and human treatment of slaves[1] and regarded their emancipation as a meritorious act.[2] Significantly, the *Quran* enjoined that the atonement for some sins consisted in manumitting slaves as also the Prophet encouraged it for the recompense of any human error one may fall into. History bears testimony to the fact that, as a result of the Prophet's role, the attitudes of Arab tribes towards slavery underwent such a radical transformation that emancipation of slaves dominated the consciousness of the masters to the greatest degree. Following the Prophet's example, his companions set free their slaves in order to enable them to become part and parcel of the Islamic brotherhood. Abu Bakr, the first Caliph, spent huge sums of money on buying off slaves from the idolatrous chiefs of the Quraish to set them free afterwards. In setting aside the norms of slave-owning system, the Prophet married his cousin Zainab, daughter of Jansh, to his ex-slave Zaid. The exaltation of Bilal and Salman-i Farsi is too well known to merit special mention here. The appointment of slaves as military commanders was yet another radical step towards generating consciousness of oneness among the faithful. According to the most authoritative work on *hadith*, the Prophet is reported to have said: "Hear and obey (the orders of your leader) although the man appointed above you as your leader be a negro slave with a raisinlike head so long as he continues to enforce among you God's law."[3]

The Prophet endeavoured to change these ingrained attitudes in order to build up the dignity of human personality on feelings of love, mutual understanding and self-respect. The construction of the self and the conversion of soul to Islam, therefore, went hand in glove with each other. The self of the convert arose in interaction with the social and non-social environment. The social environment, of course, was important. But more important was the interaction that Islam sought at the mental and psychological level with the social environment. Islam stood for the formation of only such attitudes as involved imitating the behaviour of the Prophet rather than taking his role in history. The companions of the Prophet, including the Pious Caliphs, were far from able to match the Prophet. Following the *Sunna* signified changing one's group loyalties and servile attitudes into obedience to the leader for understanding and recognising the deeper truths about purposeful, individual and social existence. And when one develops such an attitude towards one's self, one is worth something no matter what one's position in society. The history of the evolution of human personalities consequent upon their conversion to Islam has been that of attitudes marked by coherence of thought and behaviour in consonance with the *Sunna*.

We have seen in the previous chapter that no individual can be compared with another in respect of his individuality.

Naturally, then, individual attitudes differ widely. At the personal level, particularly, we may argue about the attitudes of as many souls as those living on earth. However, at the social level one can reasonably talk about specific attitudes of a particular social group, community or nation. In one case, an attitude differs from personality to personality while in the other social attitudes differ from one nation to another. Viewed in this perspective the history of Islam has been that of human attitudes towards one's self and, also, one's society.

As a press photographer may catch one in the attitude of prayer or defiance, so does history catch Muslims in a variety of moods. The varied response of individuals and societies to Islam becomes comprehensible when one takes a close view of their respective psychological structures.

Let us, therefore, begin with the structures of belief and unbelief rooted in the individual and collective psyche. Before the advent of the *Quran*, Allah was not totally unknown among the Arabs. Although known to them as the supreme god, creator and sustainer of life, yet he was distant in everyday relationship or connection in their consciousness. Associated with *ilah* were three goddesses considered to be his daughters—al-Lat, Manat, and al-Uzza. They were objects of worship along with several hundred idols of tribal patron deities in the Ka'ba itself. The religious consciousness of the pagan Arabs reflected their tribal nature and social structure. The attitude towards gods and goddesses and their spirits, pervading stones, trees, springs and wells, was that of fear and respect rather than love. Such an attitude was in conformity with the ethos of tribal authority and loyalty. In the midst of the objects of cultic rituals (sacrifice, pilgrimage, prayer) of supplication and propitiation celebrated at local shrines, the tribal chiefs struck an attitude of fear and respect with the purpose of fostering tribal ties of group loyalty or solidarity, as the fountainhead of power for a clan or tribe. This attitude was also necessitated by the absence of a central authority or law both in religious and political terms.

It follows that tribal religion had no or very little sense of cosmic moral purpose or of individual or communal responsibility. The sole aim of individual existence was preservation of tribal and familial ties. Chivalry, loyalty and fealty to family and tribal chief, use of brutal strength for the protection of tribal solidarity against an imminent threat or group vendetta were the dominant characteristics of the social structure. The concept of justice was embedded in the tribal morality granting licence for revenge or retaliation in the face of the threats to the very existence of tribe. In sum, then, the tribal religious attitudes were geared to the ethnocentric belief of preserving tribal and family honour. The only consciousness that permeated the minds of individuals was that of tribal experience or custom. The *summum bonum* of life was not the spirit of enquiry after religious or mundane truth but habitual acquiescence in the tribal ethical code or value system.

Although superbly humble and amiable in human relations, the Prophet did not have an acquiescent nature in the context of the oppressive social order. As a matter of reality, his life before the advent of the *Quran* was characterised by a spirit of revolt against the slavish ideal of acquiescence in obnoxious social norms. Conversely, the *status quo* was only acceptable to tribal groups since it suited the egocentricity of their leaders. Although Muhammad belonged to a respectable tribe, yet he was neither class-conscious nor egoistic. Far from throwing in his lot with the emerging oligarchy within the tribe, he preferred to lead an austere life in the face of the growing disparity between the rich and the poor. His seclusion in the cave, apart from his spiritual moorings, reflected the period of inner struggle against the hierarchical social order for vindicating the right of every individual to happiness. Thus while disregarding his own self-interest and the interests of his social group in the modern sense, Muhammad's *Sunna* evolved a principle of life and a moral quality which characterised him distinctively from the standpoint of his attitude to society and people. It was this altruism—combined with perseverance, determined spirit, right mental and moral excellence—that have always determined the attitudes of many known and unknown great men of Islamic history. Here an attempt will be made to reflect on some dominant attitudes.

The attitudes of the immediate followers of Muhammad deserve careful consideration. Among them particular mention must be made of Abu Bakr, Umar, Uthman and Ali, well known as rightly guided caliphs *(Khulafa-i-Rashidun)*. Despite their closeness to the Prophet and positions of power and authority, their attitude towards life was one of simple dignity and austerity. Their attitude towards the problems of life, together with six other named companions, was "acknowledged by the Prophet as the closest approximation to the ideal Muslim". The ten companions were promised paradise: "My companions are even as the stars: whomsoever of them you follow, you shall be rightly guided".

The righteous caliphs appeared to many a Muslim mystic of history to be true embodiments of the *Sunna* of the Prophet. Al-Kharraaz, renowned Sufi of the third/ninth century, observes thus:

> When Abu Bakr succeeded to the leadership, and the world in its eternity came to him in abasement, he did not lift up his head on that account, or make any pretensions; he wore a single garment, which he used to pin together; so that he was known as the 'man of two pins'. 'Umar b. al-Khattab, who also ruled the world in its entirety, lived on bread and olive-oil; his clothes were patched in a dozen places, some of the patches being of leather; and yet there were opened unto him the treasures of Chosroes and Caesar. As for 'Uthman, he was like one of his slaves in dress and appearance; of him it is related that he was seen coming out of one of his gardens with a faggot of firewood on his shoulders, and when questioned on the matter he said, 'I wanted to see whether my soul would refuse'. When Ali succeeded to the rule he bought a waistband for four dirhams and a shirt for five dirhams; finding the sleeve of his garment too long, he went to a cobbler and taking his knife cut off the sleeve level with the tops of his fingers; yet this same man divided the world right and left.[4]

Stories about the asceticism of the four caliphs in the literature on Islamic mysticism are many. The mystic attitude towards Islam was based on a deep understanding of the *Quran* in conjunction with the sayings of the Prophet (*hadith*). What is, however, important to remember is that most *ahadith* which suited the Sufi view of Islam were not considered to be authentic and rejected by al-Bukhari (d. 256/870) and Muslim (d. 261/875). Does this mean that the Sufi tradition in Islam has very weak theological foundations? This question is crucial to our understanding of two basic attitudes of Muslims, namely, theological and mystical.

In terms of history, it is not theology but the life of Muhammad that provides us keys to an objective understanding of the culmination of *din* in his supernal personality and social role. The fundamental argument of the *Quran* is directed against dogmatism and particularism of the Jewish and Christian theological ethnocentrism *vis-a-vis Tawhidic* universalism. While theology tends to make religion somewhat an isolated phenomenon in history, the Quranic *Weltanschauung* relates religion to an individual's inner strivings, emotive and mental attitudes, and also to his social and ecological environment. Islam has been appropriately called *din al-fitra*[5] which carries a much broader sense of its comprehensiveness and adaptiveness rather than narrowness and exclusiveness in any social setting. The spread of Islam has abundantly been a fact of social rather than mere religious history. The very terms religious, spiritual or mystical make no sense to me if not related to social.

The main difference between the Sufi and theological approaches to Islam is that of attitudes rather than difference in kind. Theology in Islam began to assume importance, particularly, following scholarly attempts at studying *hadith*. A great deal of controversy existed on various questions of social importance, each group invoking *hadith* to support its rival claims. Amidst acrimonious debate, works of monumental significance on the *hadith* were produced by al-Bukhari and Muslim. The acknowledged theologians and lawyers of the time were undoubtedly impressed by the methodology adopted for examining the authenticity of the *hadith*. Bukhari, for instance, "selected out the 600,000 traditions he collected from 1,000 Sheikhs in the course of sixteen years of travel and labour in Persia, al-Iraq, Syria, al-Hijaz and Egypt some 7275".[6] Consequently, Muslim scholarship not only laid the foundation of the science of *hadith* but, simultaneously, opened the door for further research for testing the genuineness of the utterances of Muhammad. But it must be pointed out that in their noble aim of establishing the genuineness of the *hadith*, scholars even went to the extent of casting doubt on such *ahadith* as were not in conflict with the spirit of the Quranic teachings. Such utterances of the Prophet, however, were of central importance for the Sufis considering their attitudes towards poverty and riches.

By the time the science of *hadith* was put on a firm footing by al-Bukhari and Muslim, Sufism had taken deep roots. Since the asceticism of the early Sufis had become an established fact, it was not looked on with favour by the people, who wanted a clear exposition of truth in orderly propositions. Islam for them was not simply knowledge of God, but more importantly, right living and right thinking on the basis of ideas of truth, classified and arranged. However, in applying the science of the mind to the utterances of the Prophet, scholars seem to have been influenced by utilitarian rather than mere religious considerations. For example, they saw in the asceticism of the early Sufis certain characteristics akin to renunciation of Christian monks disapproved in the *Quran*. The reasons for rejection of such *ahadith* "poverty is my pride" and the like can be better imagined than described considering the theological emphasis on the social and moral development of the *umma* on a set of beliefs and principles. The real foundation of authoritative works on *hadith* like Bukhari's is to be sought in the attitude of mind which determined the methods of examining the authencity of *hadith* for the pragmatic interests of *din*. Viewed against this background, the general theological emphasis on conforming one's behaviour to the *hadith* as contained in authoritative works alone sounds not only mechanical but also unwarranted, both from religious and historical standpoints.

Muhammad and the *Quran* have undoubtedly left a more indelible mark on the history of the world than any historical figure or divine book. Notwithstanding an aura of holiness surrounding the Prophet and eternal immutability of the Divine commands, both Allah and Muhammad have remained impregnable forces of history to this day. Two points of vital social significance lend weight to the historical objectivity underlying our argument. First, before the advent of the *Quran*, Muhammad was not a Prophet of legend but of history. Born with an aristocratic lineage, the solitary living of the orphan was evident in his wanderings over the hills about Mecca and the tending of the family's flocks. As the boy entered into adulthood, his manhood—moral excellence, compassion, scrupulousness in business dealings, sagacity, friendliness and even living in relative solitude—earned him the title of *al-Amin* in *Jahilyya*. Second, the *Quran* was not revealed to the Prophet in mysterious circumstances, notwithstanding his initial experience at Hira, but as a matter of objective reality, the abiding social relevance of its teachings was brought home to mankind in the manifestation and exemplification of his historical role. Although the critics of Islam recognise the central role of the *Quran* and the Prophet in history, yet there is a marked degree of sadism in their ingrained habit of drawing a red herring across the trail. Thus, in their concerted attempts to present a distorted view of Islam, they have drawn heavily on the debate that has been natural to the development of theology in Islam in latter-day history. I would, therefore, have recourse to the *Quran* in respect of such *ahadith* as do not find mention in the authoritative works. Since the *Quran* encourages thinking concordant with its Mind it would also be of some value to probe beyond the reason of classical compilers of *ahadith*.

Most Sufis have always taken pride in quoting the *hadith* 'poverty is my pride' to justify their aversion for riches in preference to self-imposed poverty *(faqr)*. Judged by the *Quran's* disapproval of the human tendency to amass worldly possessions,[7] this *hadith* cannot be rejected. Not only is the tone and tenor of the *Quran* directed against material pursuits and pleasures, but the river-like generosity of the Prophet, his concern for the sufferings of the poor and weak, and his abstemious habits provide sufficient proof for the originality of the *hadith* extolling poverty. Another saying attributed to the Prophet is in the form of prayer: "O God, make me live lowly and die lowly and rise from the dead among the lowly." He also said, "On the Day of Resurrection God will say, 'Bring ye My loved ones nigh unto Me'; then the angels will say, 'Who are Thy loved ones?' and God will answer them, saying, 'The poor and destitute'."[8]

Although there is evidence to show that the Prophet sought the refuge of Allah against destitution, yet there is no reason to believe that he wanted his followers to lead a life of ease, luxury and comfort. What is remarkable about his life is that the commercial prosperity of Mecca together with the great power and overflow of riches which accrued to Islam in the later days of his mission, did not have the slightest effect on his austere habits. But for this reason his self-imposed poverty and that of his four illustrious companions, particularly Ali, would not have been eulogised in the Islamic literature and lore. Notwithstanding the undisputed fact of the avowal of poverty as a virtue by the

Prophet—reflected in his abstemiousness, tattered clothes and living conditions of the household—two dominant attitudes about wealth have been discernible in the Muslim society from very early days of Islam.

The Quran, the *Sunna* of the Prophet and also the example of his four companions had a very vast potential for prompting Muslim thinkers to propound an egalitarian social philosophy within the Islamic framework. Strangely enough, it was not the socio-economic but metaphysical, eschatological and political issues that preoccupied the minds of the early theologians of Islam. The extremist views of the Kharijites on the legitimacy of 'Uthman to rule and Ali's acceptance of arbitration at the hands of Muawiyah and later the Mutazila's "dogmatic intolerance" against moderate attitude of Ahmad ibn Hanbal provided solid foundations for the development of theology in Islam as a scientific discipline at the cost of what may be termed "Islamic Economics". The Sufis who were deeply conscious of the growing economic disparities between the rich and the poor in Muslim societies could not make any meaningful contribution towards narrowing down the gulf between the "haves" and "have-nots". The Sufis' glorification of poverty, notwithstanding their acute sense of social justice as enshrined in the *Quran* and the *Sunna*, provided sufficient ground and climate for the masses to acquiesce in a predetermined fate or social position in a given socio-political order. Sufis were not extremists; moderation was the keynote of their teachings. Yet it must be admitted that their social attitudes and institutions were responsible more for buttressing the concept of a sort of parallel government, spiritual territories *(wilaya)*, within the spiritual and temporal phenomena than for evolving and fostering the idea of a welfare state within an objective social order. Consequently, the Sufis gave a long rope to the *ulama-i-duniyya* or *ulama-i-su* in strengthening their position as co-sharers of the state power, based more on the political exigencies of the time rather than on the principles of the *Shari'a*. The Sufis, of course, can claim the merit of combating and conquering worldly ambition; yet in this superb personal achievement one cannot fail to see elements stultifying the flowering of any thinking towards the growth of a viable economic and political structure based on the spiritual ethics of the *Quran* and the *Sunna*.

Moderation, the cardinal teaching of the *Quran,* and in fact the inseparable companion of the Prophet's wisdom, has not very often remained the watchword of Muslim societies. Instead, in its historical manifestations, Islam came to be recognised as something sensational.[10] At no stage in the history of its revelation has the *Quran* urged the Prophet to go beyond the bounds of moderation. As a matter of fact, the Prophet's *Sunna* was the meeting ground of both divine and human wisdom. Contrary to this, most theologians and thinkers of Islam adopted particular attitudes in their socio-historical and political settings almost to the point of no return. The Kharijite and Mutazila reaction, for instance, was not without some religious basis, but extremism of every kind, repeatedly disapproved in the *Quran,* consigned their rationale to the dustbin of history.

Ever since the advent of the *Quran,* Islam's insistence has been on unerring belief *(iman)* and right action *(ihsan).* Both are so intertwined that it would be absurd to categorise Islam either as "orthodox" or "orthoprax". Notwithstanding Orientalist attempts in that direction[11], it may be observed that there is an inherent danger in overemphasizing the importance of one term over the other. Had Islam been simply a matter of belief or faith, there would have been no need for right action or practice in history; and had it been a question of orthopraxy, or correct action, Islam would have merely assumed the form of a code of conduct or a way of life. From the standpoint of the *Quran,* however, Islam is exclusively neither of the two. To say that Islam is simply a matter of belief is tantamount to reducing it to an abstraction and to think that it simply means surrender to the will of Allah would amount to amputating mind from the human body.

What, then, provides a nexus between belief and right action? The answer is simple: the never-ceasing consciousness within ourselves in relation to our faith and behaviour. Awareness or consciousness of shaping one's individual actions in the mould of the *Sunna* as a basis for peaceful and meaningful existence in this world and as a prologue to a much better life in the Hereafter thus form the substratum of truth underlying the Islamic faith. Every individual action should spring from faith; and a true believer's constant endeavour should be to improve the quality of his faith by recognising the reality of the Prophet's

Sunna in his own everyday growing moral rectitude. Deeply conscious of the fact that he can never come up to his ideal standard, yet it has been the marked trait of a believer's personality not so much to actualise the highest standard of the Prophet's human excellence but to realise and immortalise it in his conscious act of imitating the patterns of the *Sunna*. Further, repeated daily recitation of benediction (*durud* or *as-salat*) and prayer for granting "a glorious station" to Muhammad in his conscious act of imitating the patterns of the *Sunna* not only rouse primeval spiritual yearnings in him, but more importantly, form a primer of self-regeneration on a sound spiritual, social and intellectual understanding. Not only the daily recitation of the *adhan*, and the *Quran*, but, also, that of *na't* in mellifluous tones bring a certain degree of comfort to a believer's heart and life in the welter of everyday interrelated and unrelated facts of social existence. The meaning and aim of Islam, then, is obedience to Allah and Muhammad[12] in improvement of self and benevolence to men[13] in the totality of spiritual and social consciousness characterised by unerring faith and right action or practice in congruity with the spirit of the *Quran* and the *Sunna*. Seen in the normative (spiritual) and historical perspective, conversion to Islam does not mean a sudden turnover from unbelief to belief in the immutability of certain dogmas, but a matter of everyday individual experiences, attitudes and transmutations at a snail's pace.

Orthodoxy, then as understood in Christian sense, is alien to Islam. Since there is a strong element of dogmatism in orthodoxy, this is the reason that the Sufis rejected it strictly from the Quranic standpoint. The Quranic concept of three conditions of the human soul—*ammara*[14], *lawwama*[15] and *mutma'ina*[16], superbly discussed in Sufi literature and lore, is enough to dispel any doubt about the supposed dogmatism of basic Islamic beliefs. Being *din al-fitra*, the *Quran* gives utmost importance to imperfections of the human mind in an imperfect world of the Creator's own creation. Naturally, then, human attitudes towards the realisation of the Will of Allah differ from one believer to another and from one group to another. Islam, thus understood, reserves final judgment on human conduct for Allah alone: "Say everyone acts according to his own disposition. But your Lord knows who it is that is best guided on the Way".[17]

Notes and References

1. *Quran*, 16/71.
2. Ibid., 90/13; 58/3.
3. *Muqadima Tajrid al-Bukhari*, original Arabic text with Urdu translation. Malik Din Mohammad and Sons Publishers, Lahore, p. 994.
4. Kharraz, *Kitab al-Sidiq*, tr. Arberry, pp. 20-21, quoted in A.J. Arberry, *Sufism*, London, 1990, p. 32.
5. "So set thou face truly to the religion being upright, the nature in which Allah has made mankind. There is no altering (the laws of) Allah's creation. That is the right religion, but most men know not". *Quran*, 30/30. Although the true nature of man is good considering his creation in the best of moulds, he loses his identity as God's vicegerent in pursuit of his mere worldly ambitions. Thus while man's tendency to cling to the earth is not unnatural, his intuitive ability to restore human nature to what it should be under the Will of Allah is superbly natural. And this is possible only when he reflects on his puny existence in relation to his Creator.
6. Hitti, *History of the Arabs*, p. 395.
7. *Quran*, 3/14; 43/35; 102/1-8; 104/2-3; 51/19; 70/24-25; 11/87; 2/270-271, 274-275; 30/38-39; 92/11. On the abuse of wealth, see Ibid., 3/185, 197;4/77, 9/38; 10/23, 70, 28/60; 30/7; 40/39; 42/36; 53/29; 107/1-7.
8. Ali Hujwiri, *Kashf al-mahjub*, tr. Nicholoson, p.19.
9. Abu Daud and An-Nasai, quoted in Yusuf al-Qardawi, *Mushkilat al-faqr wa kaifa alijaha at-Islam,* Urdu tr. under the title *Islam mean garibi ka ilaj*, Dr. al-Salfia, Bombay, 1981.
10. Arnold Toynbee remarks that four "Higher Religions" correspond to basic psychological types. The dominant characteristic of Hinduism is thinking, of Christianity-feeling, of Islam sensation, of Buddhism-intuition. See Arnold Toynbee, *A Study of History*, London, 1934-54, Vol. VII, p. 716. The universal church that is to embrace the world, is not, in Toynbee's plan, to emerge as syncretism but rather as "the symbiosis of the Higher Religions" that grew upon the foundation of the "Secondary Civilization". However, Hugh Trevor-Roper, the Oxford historian, rightly describes Toynbee's new religion as merely mish-mash. See Trevor Roper, "Arnold Toynbee's Millenium", *Encounter*, June, 1957.
11. Cantewell Smith, *Islam in Modern History*, p. 28; Fazlur Rahman, Islam, 2nd ed., Chicago, 1979, p. 91.
12. *Quran*, 64/12; See also 48/10, 18.
13. *Khair al-nas man yanfa al-nas.*

14. *Quran*, 12/53.
15. Ibid., 75/2.
16. Ibid., 89/27.
17. Ibid., 17/84.

6

ISLAM AND SOUTH ASIAN MUSLIM SOCIETIES

The Indian subcontinent has never been a monolithic entity in strict political and cultural terms. Historians stress the political unification of the subcontinent during the periods of the great empires—the Mauryas, the Guptas and the Mughals. True, the existence of such empires aimed at checking centrifugal forces and introducing uniformity in administration, but the fact remains that even such powerful governments could not totally obliterate the identity and assertiveness of cultural zones within the boundaries of their seemingly unified political structure. Notwithstanding the stark sensitivity of certain regions of the subcontinent about historical and cultural distinctiveness, the state power has always been wont to ignore this crucial heritage. Kashmir and Bangladesh, to mention only the most important regions, survive as distinct cultural entities as they existed centuries before. Each of these regions has a glorious heritage to be proud of. Whatever their affiliations, Hindus and Muslims living in these regions have seldom ceased to assert their selfhood in terms of Kashmiris and Bengalis. A keen observer has rarely failed to notice something problematic about their identity, thinking and social behaviour. In the post-partition period a sense of the loss of historical and cultural identity has existed in acute forms, particularly among Bengalis and Kashmiri Muslims. While behind the emergence of Bangladesh, historical, geographical and cultural factors played an important part, almost similar pattern cannot be ruled out in studying the Kashmir imbroglio.

Where does, then, Islam figure in the struggle of the Kashmiri Muslims for preserving their historical and cultural identity? Although this question needs a detailed discussion than the one attempted here, nevertheless, a few observations may be made within our specific context.

Kashmir is undoubtedly South Asia's most strategic and sensitive region in political, religious and cultural terms. Since the emergence of political consciousness among its Muslim inhabitants after centuries of misrule in 1930s, the Valley's history has followed a broader, slower rhythm of religio-cultural conjunctures in all its contemporary manifestations rather than that of the event. True, modern or so to say, Western education has brought about many changes in the pattern of social life, but it must be remembered that such changes have been synchronous with the valley's long history. Studied in totality, social reality, though always in a flux, has repeated details of innumerable previous realities. Around several organised and unorganised zones enveloping social life, Islamic influence always makes its presence felt. The evolution of Kashmiri Muslim society has thus to be explained in the context of its own time. It is indeed a 'child of its time', the expanse of time surrounding it in the very spirit of its recurrent response to Islam. The spirit of historical time needs to be defined within the context of a relationship that Islam has been seeking to establish with Kashmir's history, culture and ecology over centuries of its acculturative and assimilative process. Consequently, Kashmiri literature and lore have, always orchestrated the music of a consciousness characteristic of a recurrent phase of social evolution in which, to borrow the phraseology of Marc Bloch "society contemplates its own image".[1] So indelible has been the influence of Islam on the evolution of Kashmiri language that the litterateurs of the contemporary social scene continue to resist attempts at obliterating their religious and cultural identity. It has elsewhere been shown that Islam and mundane situations seem to coalesce rather than conflict, in the ongoing social drama in Kashmir.[2]

Islam is thus not just a thing built, put together; neither is it an ideological construct in the strictest sense of the revelation and the *Sunna*. It is poles apart from an ideology or, more than that, strikingly different from that division itself and more profound in the details of its endless and inexhaustible history of structures and group of structures owing existence to their contact with Islam. There is no unilateral history of Islam considering fundamental paradoxes and contradictions of human life and nature. It is, indeed, hazardous to confine our thinking within modern definitions of Islam and its followers since they make a fetish of the dichotomy between belief and practice. To understand Islam it is necessary to dive beneath definitions.

Islam knows no definition. And, if at all, any human definition may be acceptable to Allah, it would be nothing short of how a believer moulds his social behaviour in consonance with the spirit of the *Quran* and the *Sunna*. Islam has to be lived, practised, felt, experienced and, not the least, debated in the recesses of the mind in close relationship with one's soul and heart. The multiplicity of attitudes among Muslims is, therefore, comprehensible, and so is the diversity of Muslim societies within their varied historical, geographical and socio-cultural environments.

The fundamental movement of Islamic history today is therefore not one of selecting between this or that attitude but of accepting and absorbing all the successive attitudes in which one after another there have been attempts to confine it. Doesn't every attitude spring from one's own understanding of Islam?

It is not therefore difficult to understand why over several centuries the concept of the *umma* as a political entity has not remained more than a cherished ideal. Undoubtedly the ideal flourished during the heyday of the pious Caliphate. Despite the bloodshed and hair-splitting controversies characterising the caliphal period of Uthman and Ali, the personal piety of the caliphs proved to be a potent force in reinforcing the idea of a welfare state based intrinsically on the concept of the *umma's* spiritual and social unity fostered by individual character. With Muawiya's decision to nominate Yazid as his successor the history of Islam took a different course. There is no greater rupture with the concept of the unity of the *umma* anymore than the one that we find in Yazid's succession to the *Khilafa*. But then the martyrdom of Husain provides a unique example of attesting to the historic vindication of the unity of the *umma* embedded deeply in the Quranic consciousness of personal piety, struggle and sacrifice rather than in the superficial struggle for capturing power *(daula)* for enforcing the *Shari'a* of Allah. Husain's struggle was not prompted by any political ambition but by the very prospect of the *ummas'* acquiescence in the authority of a villain as its leader. And what made Husain challenge the authority of Yazid was his strict adherence to the *Sunna* of his grandfather. Muawiya had departed from the *Sunna* in respect of introducing the *bid'a* of hereditary succession; hence the *Sunna* demanded the vindication of its essential spirit on the part of none other than al-i Muhammad themselves.

Muhammad, as the leader of the *umma*, had organised the flowering of spiritual values into a single historical destiny through coherent succession of phases. This is the reason that history has shown time and again the *Sunna's* greater relevance as a vital social force than any worldly ideology. This great structure of Islam has travelled through vast tracts of time and regions without changing its essential spirit; its abiding value for true believers has always been in their consciousness to live within the widening and encompassing horizons of its sequential and seminal spirituality and sociology. The history of Islam and the evolution of Muslim societies has revolved round the role of creative personalities rooted in the *Sunna*.

Muslim societies are marked by their common characteristics and internal contradictions. They have their own borders, centres, peripheries and their provinces. There are general as well as particular forms. Remarkably they survive political, social, economic and even ideological upheavals. Occasionally, upheavals are the result of constellation of a number of forces other than purely religious. But even in such circumstances Islam does not cease to play its historical role. It is in this sense that the concept of the *umma* continues to survive as a solidifying force among Muslims worldwide.

What does the concept of the *umma* stand for? Does it stand for the conquest of the world? Does it aim at waging an incessant battle for the fruition of its ideal of establishing *Khilafa* throughout the world?

Umma is primarily a universal ideal in the Quranic sense. Although its historical and germinal locus was Arabia, it did not confine itself within a precise area. The 'diffusion' of its features or elements in the non-Arab world was the inevitable result of a historical process. However, it would be too bold to assert that transmission of the Islamic ideal sounded the disaster or death of various cultures. The 'diffusion' of Islamic civilisation did not necessarily cause total collapse or disintegration of local cultures; it set in motion such forces as created favourable conditions for the convergence of several diverse elements. In spite of the fact that Islamic monotheism, spiritualism and egalitarianism were diametrically opposed to Zoroastrianism, Buddhism, Hinduism and animism, yet the human effort was ever inclined to meet at a certain point of understanding. But for this convergence of attitudes, Islamic civilisation would not have developed amidst the survival of ancient religions and cultures in accordance with the purpose of creation.

Convergence is a better term than syncretism[3] for understanding the history of the evolution of Muslim societies. The latter concept has almost assumed the force of law in Orientalism. That a sensitive Muslim scholar like Akbar S. Ahmad has also sought to discover Islam in the pigeon holes of Western models is shown in his attempt at dramatising the polarity between the so-called "Orthodox" Islam and "Syncretist" Islam in his assessment of Aurangzeb, Dara Shikoh or Zia-ul-Haque and Bhutto. Ahmad approvingly uses such Orientalist terminologies as "mystical" and "informal Islam" to designate the quality of faith of individual Muslims.[4] Although such comparisons are faulty in several respects, they do bring home to us the importance of a methodology, alien to Islam, for understanding Islam through syncretic category of thought. The persistence of application of the syncretic model is attributable to the evolution of the one whole—the composite Indian culture—in Indian historiography. The evolution of the synthetic Indian culture is said to have resulted during long centuries of Islamic presence in the subcontinent. Tara Chand, a reputed and enlightened historian, promoted the cause of national integration on syncretic model.[5] But such a model is no more than a product of the mind of an historian obsessed with serving the nationalist goals in Indian historiography. Annemarie Schimmel goes several steps further in encapsulating Islam in two categories, viz., "mystico-syncretistic" and "Prophetic-separatist" on the premise of the twentieth century politics of the Muslims of subcontinent. While the former represents, argues Schimmel, the ethos of the syncretic culture of Indian Muslims, the latter concept that of the separatist ideology of the Muslims of Pakistan.[6] Seen in this perspective, one may reasonably ask whether a Muslim of the Bhutto type has any right to live in Pakistan. Whatever the merit of syncretism in the sociology of religion in Western social sciences, its use seems to me of a lesser value in comparison with the method of historical analysis and synthesis inspired by the *Quran*.

The merging of two or more inflectional categories in any social environment is ascribable to the reconciliation or union of different or opposing principles and practices. Such a process, even if it exists in superficialities of our minds, seems to me formidably more mysterious than the inscrutable ways of providence. Being myself rooted in the *Sunna* and Sufism, I find it difficult to reconcile myself with the idea of equating the *Sunna* with separatists' political ideology and syncretism with the followers of the Sufis. Both syncretism and separatism are social and historical processes, embedded neither in the *Quran* nor in the *Sunna*. Separatism is tantamount to isolationism and syncretism is always bound to create distortion and confusion of the worst type. The *Quran* was revealed with the purpose of raising man on to the highest pedestal of learning and empathic understanding of the social environment. The *Quran* favours a middle course[7] rather than an extreme position even in matters of belief[8] and practice.[9] The only objective reality in terms of the *Quran* is diversity of human beliefs[10] rather than their unity. And the only unity in diversity the *Quran* speaks of is with reference to attitudes. That is, man is inclined to follow a course quite contrary either to the universal reason of the *Quran* or in congruence with its pristine spirit. For example, when the *Quran* allows polygamy and divorce, it does not make it binding on the believer to have recourse to such practices in any ritual sense. Such concessions have been granted in exceptional circumstances, not as a rule, but considering social and economic conditions and specificity of certain individual dispositions. Likewise, when the *Quran* invites people to Islam, it does not make surrender to Allah's will a matter of mere ritual performances but a continuous striving of the soul, heart, mind and behaviour in relation to one's social environment. Islam is thus not a matter of dramatic and wholesale conversions but a never-ceasing process in the movement of individuals and societies. While Islam is a perfect religion in the model of the Prophet's *Sunna* and in his ideal society, the historical movement of several societies exposed to its radiance cannot be unilinear. The seemingly syncretic or synthetic character of Muslim societies has therefore various nuances rather than generally accepted conceptual connotations in the Western social sciences. Let me illustrate the point with reference to the shrine of Hazratbal in the Kashmir Valley.[11]

Being a repository of the sacred hair of the Prophet Muhammad, the shrine attracts not less than ten thousand Muslims on Fridays and nearly hundred thousand Muslims on the eve of *Miraj al-Nabi* and *Milad al-Nabi*. The anniversaries of *Khulafa-i-Rashidun* are also celebrated at Hazratbal with traditional fervour. On such occasions the sacred hair is exhibited in the midst of a huge crowd chanting *durud* and litanies. One marked trait of most Kashmiri Muslims has been the practice of invoking the help of Allah and the Prophet with folded hands in their enterprises of spiritual and social nature. The loud chanting of an invocatory prayer, largely based on the *Quran* and *hadith*, with an emotional and devotional fervour and tone is the usual sight at such gatherings.

The indigenous ritual behaviour of Kashmiri Muslims, at various shrines and mosques, in addition to Hazratbal, has been viewed by many an outside observer as an assimilation of Islam into the ancient Hindu-Buddhist environment of the Valley. At the early stage of religious and historical consciousness striking similarities—veneration of the relic in a manner of the ancient Buddhist practice of worshipping the tooth of Buddha in the Valley and its exhibition at an ancient site in Srinagar, singing of *na't* and *manjat* in chorus resembling loud chanting of litanies in Hindu temples, focus of Muslims on the repository of the relic in the shrine itself with folded hands—were drawn by me to convince myself as to how Islam in the Valley had compromised with local practices in order to ensure its viability in syncretic and synthetic forms. Having listened for over two decades to religious discourses from the *Jamat-i-Islami* and particularly *Ahl-i Hadith* in denunciation of what they regard as deviations in the Islam of Kashmiris, the ritual behaviour of my compatriots appeared at one stage to me to be *bid'a*. But as my spiritual and historical consciousness grew in the comparative perspectives and environment of various mosques and shrines in a spirit of enquiry, the objective reality about the movement of Islam in the orderly evolution of Muslim societies began to dawn upon me in consonance with their spatio-temporal dimensions. As a matter of fact, the Kashmiris, even after their 'conversion' to Islam could not avoid retaining the essential elements of the local ancient religious culture and ethos while adapting to Islamic forms of life and worship. Thus the convergence[12] of Islam and historical circumstances emboldens us to assume that the beliefs comprising a given culture have important functions for the social structure and personality of the people and, indeed, continue to survive in spite of seemingly great historical upheavals. The objective fact is that the historian can never get away from the timeless realms of spiritual and social consciousness or, simply, from the question of time in history. The historian who is himself both an inside and outside observer in addition to being a participant in the ritual function cannot but formulate such ideas as are opposed to stereotypes. The great social edifice of Hazratbal has evolved out of the interaction between Islam and society; it cannot envisage the religious life of Kashmiri Muslims as a mechanism that can be stopped at leisure in order to reveal frozen images of the unimaginative and zealous reformers including social scientists whose conclusions are intrinsically rooted in the stereotypical images rather than an indepth enquiry into a participation in the spiritual and social phenomena. The social significance of the shrine is centred round the deeper levels of spirituality, historicity, mentalities, sensitivity, sociability, temporality, and the *Tawhidic* universalism of Muslim societies.

Seen in comparative perspectives, the shrine of Hazratbal is superimposed in the consciousness of Kashmiri Muslims as a historical and symbolic link between Kashmir and Mecca. True, an individual focus may be on the object of veneration (sacred relic), but it is the eternal radiance of Muhammad rather than the worship of the relic that permeates his consciousness. In fact, the desire to perform the congregational prayer in the solemn and sublime environment of the historic mosque of Hazratbal is never quenched and the only conclusion is the holy Ka'ba itself which forms the chief object of pilgrims' veneration at Hazratbal. That a visit to the shrine would, at least, have reduced in the Kashmiri's religious consciousness (the apparent difference of) the physical barriers between the Arab and the 'Ajam is reflected in the following Kashmiri verses:

Whosoever has seen the sacred hair of Muhammad,
Has had in reality the vision of the Prophet.
Although he is entombed in Arabia,
His sacred hair sanctifies the *'Ajam*
He reveals the eternal reality of his radiance

only to those in Kashmir
Who have an abiding faith and are spiritually
    illuminated.[13]

Scholars have been invariably using such terms as "Kashmiri
Islam", "Indian Islam", "Indonesian Islam", "African Islam", and
so on to show the striking differences between "Arab Islam" and
the so-called regional variants of Islam. While "Arab Islam" is
considered to be rooted in "Orthodoxy", "Prophetical structure"
and "Prophetic separatist" behaviour, the regional Islam of the
non-Arab world is described as a synthesis of Islamic and
indigenous practices of various cultural zones. The Western
conceptual model of the Great Tradition and the Little Tradition
has generally been applied to explain the absorption of Islam in
the Little Tradition of the folk in contrast to a minority of religious
leaders rooted in or wedded to the Great Tradition. Islam thus
ceases to be a religion or religious force; it is religious syncretism
and cultural synthesis, effected by a process of accommodation,
adjustment and historical compulsions, that assumes the
importance of universal application and relevance in Islamic
studies. And instead of promoting a better understanding of
Islam *vis-a-vis* the historical evolution of Muslim societies in a
much broader context of the *Quran*, Orientalists have often
described the spread of Sufi movements in the non-Arab regions
as cultural rather than religious phenomena. Didn't the Sufi
leaders of the main orders trace their spiritual genealogy to
Muhammad? Wasn't Sufism born within the bosom of Islam in
the Arab world itself? Although such questions have been
favourably and convincingly answered by some Orientalists
themselves, yet a mist of ignorance continues to pervade their
minds partly due to their roots in the Western ethos and
intellectual training, but largely owing to their inability to
understand the deeper truths behind anchoring one's thinking
and behaviour in the principles of the *Quran* and the spirit of the
Sunna. Notwithstanding the merit of Western scholarship in
provoking our thought in several respects, its interpretation of
Islam and history (with certain honourable exceptions),[14] remains
a matter of perverted judgment influenced by predilections,
hybris, ideological and intellectual considerations of creed, class
and nation.[15]

No serious attempt has been made by Muslims themselves to examine the interplay of various forces in the transition of several societies to Islam in various regions of the subcontinent. Whatever little has been written bears the influence of theoretical models of the West. At the macro level Mohammad Mujeeb,[16] Ishtiaq Husain Qureishi,[17] and Imtiaz Ahmad[18] have skilfully analysed various strands in the evolution of "Indo-Muslim society", "the Muslim Community of the Indo-Pak subcontinent" and "Muslim societies" respectively. But their wide generalisations about Islam in the subcontinent are as faulty as their selective 'facts' and methodology. While Mohammad Mujeeb and Imtiaz Ahmed cannot rise above the ties of Indian nationality and secularism, Qureishi traces the roots of Pakistan to the 'Muslim period' of Indian history. In the final analysis, intellect is made subservient to the ideological interests of the State power in both attitudes. The seminal thinker on modern political ideology, Karl Mannheim, was candid enough to acknowledge that ideology can be a "conscious political lie", notwithstanding the truth underlying his statement that it is "the outlook inevitably associated with a given historical and social situation and the *Weltanschuung* and style of thought bound up with it."[19] Seen in this perspective, attempts at secularising or Islamising the history of subcontinental Muslim societies are in basic conflict with the *Tawhidic Weltanschuung* of liberating human consciousness from the tyranny of ideology.

Notes and References

1. Marc Bloch, *Feudal Society*, Eng. trans. London, 1961, p. 156.
2. Ishaq Khan, *Kashmir's Transition to Islam*, p. 107.
3. For a critical analysis of a syncretistic model *vis-a-vis* the Valley of Kashmir, see Ibid.
4. Akbar S. Ahmad, *Discovering Islam: Making a Sense of History*, Vistaar, New Delhi, 1990, pp. 83-84, 87
5. Tara Chand, *The Influence of Islam on Indian Culture*, 2nd Ed. Allahabad, 1963.
6. Annemarie Schimmel, "Reflections on Popular Muslim Poetry", *Contribution to Asian Studies*, Vol. XVII, Leiden, E.J., Brill, 1982. p.18.
7. The *Quran* (2/143) speaks of the Muslim community as the median among the peoples of mankind *(Ummatan Wasatan)*. Allama Yusuf Ali translates it as an "*Ummat* justly balanced", and then rightly

remarks: "The essence of Islam is to avoid extravagances on either side". *The Holy Quran,* n. 143.

8. Ibid., 4/171; 5/77-81.
9. "Fight in the cause of Allah those who fight you. But do not transgress limits; for Allah loveth not transgressors", Ibid., 2/190. As Allam a Yusuf Ali comments: "War is permissible in self-defence and under well-defined limits. When undertaken it must be pushed with vigour, but only to restore peace and freedom for the worship of Allah. In any case strict limits must not be transgressed". Ibid., 204n.
10. "Verily, (the ends) ye strive for are diverse". *Quran,* 92/4.
11. This analysis of the ritual behaviour of Kashmiri Muslims in the most important shrine of the Valley is fresh. See also Ishaq Khan, "The significance of the Dargah of Hazratbal in the socio-economic and political life of Kashmiri Muslims", *Muslim Shrines in India,* ed. Christian W. Troll, Oxford, 1989.
12. In the article cited above I have used the term 'synthesis'.
13. Ibid.
14. See Akbar S. Ahmad, *Postmodernism and Islam: Predicament and Promise,* Penguin, 1992, pp. 179-185.
15. Edward Said, *Orientalism,* London, 1978.
16. Mohammad Mujib, *Indian Muslims,* Montreal, London, 1969.
17. Ishtiaq Hussain Qureishi, *The Muslim Community of the Indo-Pak Subcontinent, (1610-1947),* 1st Indian ed., Delhi, 1985.
18. Imtiaz Ahmad (ed.), *Caste and Social Stratification among Indian Muslims in India; Idem, Kinship and Marriage among Muslims in India; Ritual and Religion among Muslims in India.*
19. The *Quran* is neither ideological nor Utopian in thought. Since both ideology and Utopia distort the relative rather than the notional reality of this world and eternity, this is the reason that they fit nowhere into our perspective, namely, spiritio-historical. While, according to Karl Mannheim, ideology conceals reality, Utopia transgresses its limits. Mannheim thus comes near the idea of grasping reality as a totality, a view which entails both "the assimilation and transcendence of the limitations of a particular point of view". See Karl Mannheim, *Ideology and Utopia,* L. Wirth and E. Shills (trans.), Routledge and Kegan Paul, 1972, p. 94.

7

ISLAMISATION OF KNOWLEDGE?

The most noteworthy impact of the spread of Western education was the emergence of an educated *élite* among Muslims who successfully launched nationalist movements directed against Western imperialism. Their modes of resisting the colonial rulers were distinctly Western—newspapers, public meetings and associations, and organisations. The nationalist movements in the Indian subcontinent and the Middle East thrived on liberal and secular rather than on mere religious sentiments. The educated *élite*, rooted in Western education, were saturated with the ideas of liberty, democracy, nationalism, socialism and social reform. Although the religious leadership of Muslims of the subcontinent was the first to resist the onslaught of British imperialism, yet its efforts did not bear the desired results. The apparent failure of the *jihad* movement led by Sayyid Ahmad Shahid forced Muslim thinkers to devise a viable strategy for preserving Islamic identity in the subcontinent. Sir Sayyid Ahmad Khan's advice to Muslims to take to Western education was not the result of a defeatist mentality but a well-thought-out blueprint for enabling Muslims to stand on a firm footing in the midst of the challenges of immense magnitude to which they were exposed.

Sayyid Ahmad Khan's object was twofold. First, it was to enable Muslims to cope with Hindus whose society had already begun to experience certain changes in the field of self-discovery and reform as a result of Western education. Hindu self-awakening was by all accounts the result of socio-religious reform movements like the Brahmo Samaj and Arya Samaj. Further, Hindus were the first to join the civil service and hold positions of power and authority in the Government. The most important official decisions affecting public life had at least the support of the Hindu educated *élite*. While realising the implications of this change for the future of India, Sayyid Ahmad was prudent enough to advise Muslims to relatively cooperate with the British Government in the hope of enabling themselves to catch up with the educationally advanced community. His statement that "Hindus and Muslims are the two eyes of India" needs to be understood in the context of his broader vision to ensure a spirit of tolerance among them on the sound basis of self-discovery, reform, mutual understanding, co-existence and equity. An educationally backward community was bound to be exploited not only by the educationally advanced community but also by a vested interest among both. Second, Sayyid Ahmad was deeply conscious of the fact that the Muslim religious leadership was hardly capable of driving the British out of India. Being well-versed in the ethos of the West, he seems to have been confident that the exploiter could be beaten with a subtler rather than a deadly weapon. His plea for the learning of English and the acquisition of Western knowledge and acceptance of Western values was actually prompted by a statesman-like vision of preparing Muslims for a meaningful, positive and creative struggle in a changing world. One shudders at the very idea of the fate of Muslims had they not heeded the advice of Sayyid Ahmad Khan.

However, in his thought-provoking essay Ismail Raji al-Faruqi attributes the "epitome of Muslim Decline" to reformers like Sayyid Ahmad Khan and Muhammad Abdhu who bifurcated the educational system into two "sub-systems", one 'Modern' and the other 'Islamic![1]

He remarks about this division: "Unless it is dealt with and removed, it will continue to subvert every Muslim effort to reconstruct the *Ummah*, to enable it to carry forth the *amanah* that Allah *ta'la* has entrusted to it. Little did they realise that the alien humanities, social sciences, and indeed the natural sciences as well, were facets of an integral view of reality of life and the world, of history, that is equally alien to that of Islam. Little did they know of the fine yet necessary relation which binds the methodologies of these disciplines, their notions of truth and knowledge, to the value system of an alien world. *That is why their reforms bore no fruit.* On one hand, the stagnant quality of Islamic learning was left untouched. On the other, the added new learning never produced any excellence such as it produced in its homeland. On the contrary it made the Muslims dependent upon alien research and leadership. By its pompous claim of scientific objectivity it managed to convince them of its truth over and against the affirmation of Islam which the votaries of progress called conservative and backward."[2] (Emphasis mine).

To say that the reforms of Sir Sayyid and Abdhu did not yield any fruit is untenable in that they laid a solid foundation for provoking the thought processes of many a future thinker including al-Faruqi. While I make this criticism of a great martyr for a noble cause notwithstanding very many finer points in his argument, it is strange that when he defines a new set of objectives for the "Islamization of Knowledge", his goal does not seem to be different from Sayyid Ahmad. The objectives are:

1. "To master the modern disciplines.
2. To master the Islamic legacy.
3. To establish the specific relevance of Islam to each area of modern knowledge.
4. To seek ways for a creative synthesis between the legacy and modern knowledge.
5. To launch Islamic thought on the trajectory which leads it to fulfilment of the divine patterns of Allah (SWT).[3]"

But it is while elaborating his objectives that al-Faruqi strikes a different note. That his views smack of a political pathos is shown by his attempt to bring about political orientation of Islamic education in the face of the challenges posed to the Muslim states by the West. True, he stands for instilling the vision of Islam in the creative unity of Islamic and secular knowledge, but the passion for ideologisation of knowledge within the man-made, political, and even legal confines is more noticeable in the envisaged programme than a deeper quest for establishing meaningful interaction between Islam and the social phenomena. One of the basic themes of the "Islamization of Knowledge" is not to eliminate Islam from the social consciousness of its adherents, but to reinforce such consciousness on the basis of an interpretation giving it a religio-political rather than religio-social function. It is in this sense that al-Faquqi boldly asserts: "Rightly, Muslims understand *Khilafa* as predominantly political. The *Quran* repeatedly associated *Khilafa* with establishment of political power (7.73), the reassurance of security and peace

(24.55), the vanquishing of enemies and the replacement of their regime by that of the vicegerents (7:128; 10:14; 73). Political action, i.e., participation in the political process, as in the election or *bayah* of the ruler, giving continual counsel and advice to the chief of state and his ministers, monitoring their actions, criticising and even impeaching them—all these are not only desirable, but prime religious and ethical duties. Failure to perform such duties is, as the Prophet (SAAS) said, to lapse into *Jahilyyah*."[4] Thus not only politicisation of "every Muslim" but also organisation and mobilisation of generating the *ummatic* consciousness on religio-political foundations is advocated for achieving security of life, property, 'personal honour', 'place in society' and 'economic prosperity'.[5]

What prompts al-Faruqi to promote an understanding of *Khilafa* in merely political terms is not the deeper spatiotemporal consciousness characterising the *Quran* but the contemporary division of the *umma* into some "fifty or more nation-states"[6] arrayed against one another under the impact of colonial powers. It cannot be denied that "the enemy has created hostile foreign states within the body of the *Ummah* to divert Muslim energy away from reconstruction and drain it in futile wars..."[7] But is it not out of tune with the avowed objectives of the "Islamization of Knowledge" to create an imaginary threat of the possibility of colonial powers' reoccupation of the land for its "economic, strategic and political interests."?[8] As a matter of fact, Muslim nations continue to be exploited by the West in one form or the other for such interests. In my opinion, the very strength of Western powers lies hidden in the ongoing conflict between the so-called 'secular' and the proponents of Islamic ideology in the Muslim states seeking a showdown with one another on primary issues of national and Islamic significance. The external threat does not pose so serious a challenge to undermining the strength of the *umma* as the growing schism between the exigencies of national politics and the imperatives of *jihad* movements. Further, the failure of the existing *madrasah* system of education to permit Islam to function as at least one source of national culture and social integration is at the root of the deeply-felt malaise among Muslims. Given the eternal strength of the faith of *umma* in Allah's Oneness, the *Quran*, the finality of the prophethood of Muhammad and fellowship, it is un-Islamic and even unethical to castigate Muslim's "commitment to nationalism".[9] Were not Arab nationalism, Pakistani nationalism or subcontinental Muslim nationalism in its various forms the necessary concomitants and accretions of the social and religious reform movements that arose against the onslaught of the forces of proselytisation and Westernisation?

The malaise of the *umma* since the days of colonisation of parts of the so-called Muslim world by the West has not merely been political but mostly spiritual. Although modern Muslim ideologists have been very critical of Sufism, little attention has been paid to the historic fact that it was the spiritual rather than political leadership that provided *elan* to Muslim societies during a crucial phase of their history. The destruction of the *Khilafa* of Baghdad by the Mongol marauders in 1258 proved to be a turning-point in Islamic history. Not only did it open the floodgates for weakening the concept of the *Khalifa*, based on the political prudence and expedience of Ummayad and Abbasid rulers, but it also reinforced the consciousness of certain sensitive souls about the failure of the *Khulafa* to commit themselves to the model and the ideal. This consciousness did not dominate merely the minds of the Sufis but it also characterised those of the commoners. Little wonder, then, that the Sufis assumed the role of exemplars of the Prophet Muhammad's precept and example. So long as the *Khilafa* maintained a semblance of political authority, the Sufis preferred to live in meaningful and relative seclusion. But the disenchantment created by the decline of the *Khalifa's* authority forced them to give a social orientation to their inner struggle in order to save the *umma* from spiritual doom. Under the conditions created by the Mongol invasion from the East and the military expeditions undertaken by the Christians of Europe in the eleventh, twelfth and thirteenth centuries (known as the Crusades) for the recovery of the 'Holy Land' from the Muslims, resuscitation of the pristine consciousness embodying the model and ideal was inevitable. Sufism was not therefore escapism or quietism but essentially a restatement of Islam in its spatio-temporal setting.

However, what is remarkable about Sufism is not the resurgence of Islam as a political movement of re-enactment of the *Khilafat-i-Rashida* but the revitalisation of the religio-social consciousness characterising the individual souls under the spiritual leadership of Muhammad. Sufis and a host of their followers did not construe the concept of *Khilafa* as predominantly political. Modern interpretation of a few Quranic verses has led al-Faruqi to aver that "the *Quran* repeatedly *(sic?)* associated *Khilafa* with establishment of political power." Had assumption of political authority been the aim and guiding principle of the *Quran,* in that sense, therefore, the divine political mission of subjugating the whole world would have been completed during the lifetime of the Prophet and his illustrious four companions. How is it that the perceived aim has not been achieved during the last fourteen centuries? Isn't the so-called Quranic political ideology relevant to history? Has history triumphed over the supposed political will of Allah?

Any obsession with the predominantly political character of the *Khilafa* is bound to produce a human model of contradictions. This is what characterises most dedicated political activists of Islam throughout the globe. Unlike 'progressive' or 'liberal' Muslims, most of them are not bundles of contradictions in personal life. They are as committed to the *Sunna* of Muhammad in personal life as one would have least imagined them to be in the glitter of the modern world. Their spirit of sacrifice and dedication to Islam coupled with their conformity to the *Sunna* on the one hand and to ideology on the other attract many young men towards them. But while their strength lies in rousing Muslim consciousness for the revival of the *Khilafa* or an "Islamic State" their weakness lies in their ingrained tendency to resist suggestions contrary to their ideology. Consequently, the difficulties in freeing Islam from its encasement within a "dominant" political sector continue to sap the vitality of the *umma*.

The orientation of religious education on political lines was primarily an attempt to revive the *Khilafa* not in its Quranic sense but its immediate aim was to resist the colonial powers. The politicisation of Islam was not the sudden result of the struggle against colonialism, but its roots lay embedded in the social atrophe of the *umma*. The need of the time was to provide Islam with a dynamic content severed from it by the aberrations and distortions of Sufism. With the decline of the *Khanqahs* and their conversion into centres of charlatanism, the traditional values and institutions fostered by Sufism sank into oblivion. The individual piety for strengthening social solidarity, emphasized by Sufism during a critical phase of Islamic history, was now replaced by the collective commitment to Islamic ideology. It is against this background that the role of Jamal al-Din Afghani, Muhammad Abdhu and Rashid Ridha needs to be understood.

The Ikhwan al-Muslimin in Egypt and Jamat-i Islami in the subcontinent have been committed to develop institutions and educational systems designed to produce religious leaders with what may be called an appropriate Islamic political mentality. The result of this development has been social-splintering of the *umma* in various directions. How can the religious, social and political life of the *umma* be stable within such internal divisions? The contradiction is particularly reflected in the extreme positions taken by the so-called secular political authority and its defiance by the adherents of Islamic political ideology. In a struggle seeking the divorce of politics from religion or the restoration of the political glory of Islam, education is the worst affected sector in Muslim societies. While I do not advocate the total separation of politics from religion, the only doubt that lurks in my mind is whether Islam can reconcile with cliquing, politicking and electioneering.

Given the comparative failure of the *umma* to evolve a system of education meeting the requirements of Islam and also the challenges of the changing times, conferences, seminars, classroom workshops for faculty training "recasting the disciplines, preparation of university textbooks, and creative analyses and syntheses," as suggested by al-Faruqi, are necessary for generating and enriching the Islamic consciousness. But such endeavours will not pay rich dividends unless the *umma* first decides whether its aim is the "Islamization of Knowledge" or the promotion of knowledge from various perspectives ordained by the *Quran* and the Prophet. Had Islam merely stood for the promotion of knowledge of the *Quran* in the traditional theological mould or for confining the system of education within the narrow confines of religio-political ideology, the early centuries of Islamic civilisation would not have produced such a wealth of scientific research and invention. The spirit of enquiry that guided Muslim scientists and philosophers was not due so much to Hellenic influence as it was to the repeated Quranic emphasis on the inborn faculty of man to conduct an enquiry not merely to widen the scope of cosmogony but also to invigorate belief in the oneness of the Creator of the Universe, i.e., all space, seen as well-ordered system in His timeless unicity. The Sufis in their pursuit of gaining knowledge of the Creator (*ma'rifa*) well understood this truth but given the dedication of their minds and souls to the exclusively spiritual dimension of cosmogony, they could not promote an Islamic scientific spirit among their followers.

Muhammad, as the direct recipient of divine knowledge, was able to fathom the profoundest truth that knowledge knows no bounds. This is the reason that the oft-quoted but less understood and less practised prophetic dictum enjoined believers to "seek knowledge even unto China." The Prophet's *hadith* has eternal relevance; and when we exercise our minds for understanding the deeper truth underlying this *hadith* in the context of Arabia of the Prophet's time, it opens up new vistas of research for Muslim educators including social and physical scientists.

Although the above-quoted *hadith* is not mentioned in the authoritative works of *Muhaddithun*, nevertheless, it has found currency in the Sufi literature and some modern works. Whatever may be the reason for its omission or rejection, it must be pointed out that this widely referred to *hadith* is not in conflict with the teachings of the *Quran*. We may quote only two verses relevant to our discussion, notwithstanding the importance of learning through travels emphasized in the *Quran* in a different context:

"Say: Travel through the earth and see how Allah did originate creation; so will Allah produce a later creation: for Allah has power over all things.[10]

"Do they not travel through the land, so that their hearts (and minds) may thus learn wisdom and their ears may thus learn to hear? Truly it is not the eyes that are blind, but the hearts which are in their breasts."[11]

The belief that Allah has created everything in the world calls on people to study everything. We are repeatedly asked to observe, study, reflect and probe the visible world again and again, and as thoughtfully and minutely within our capacity. However closely we observe it, we shall find no flaw in it, notwithstanding its complexity and mystery in the sense of being imperfect as compared to the Hereafter. But then one is not sure whether one would be able to understand the wonder that Allah has created around. For reality is not necessarily clear and simple for the finite mind. Inasmuch as that the reality of Allah's creation, or, for that matter, even that of an atom, assumes infinitely innumerable aspects, so an enquiry after the truth about creation involves the integration of the multiple roles of the soul, the heart and the mind. True, "the word for 'heart' in Arabic speech imports both the seat of intelligent faculties and understanding as well as the seat of affections and emotions",[12] but the most important fact worthy of reflection is that the process of creation goes on ceaselessly, for at every moment new processes are called into existence by the Eternal Creator in accordance with His natural laws.

> See they not how Allah originates creation, then repeats it: truly that is easy for Allah.[13]

The point that emerges is that travelling through the earth has both literal and symbolic meaning. And if we actually go through this wide physical expanse, there will be no limit to the growth of our understanding of the wonder upon wonders that are created and transformed in every moment of every period or age. Most visible things in the process of making, remaking and destruction are comprehensible to an observant eye; but still more things, within ourselves or outside, are far beyond our vision and ken. Thus an enquiry conducted under the guidance of the *Quran* is not in conflict with scientific enquiry. Islam, as preached by the Prophet, had no room for obscurantism and required its followers to pursue all branches of learning and science with their utmost endeavours.

Knowledge can grow and develop only in comparative perspectives. And this is the reason that the main source of universal knowledge, the *Quran*, repeatedly exhorts us to study Allah's 'signs'[14] in the natural world in a spirit of enquiry after the truth. In fact, Allah's 'signs' are not specific but universal. Allah's servant (*'abd*) is not bound by any particularity; in fact in his search for truth, the attention of his soul, heart and mind is constantly focused on the universal rather than a particular reality. Promotion of knowledge should therefore lead us not only to a deeper understanding of the Creator and the created but also to an awareness of ourselves as active agents for the cause of spreading knowledge for the universal good of mankind. As the *Quran* states:

O mankind, We have created you of a single pair, a male and female (namely, Adam and Eve); and we have constituted you into tribes and nations that you may know one another. Lo: the noblest of you, in the sight of Allah, is the best in conduct. And Allah has full knowledge and is well acquainted (with all things).[15]

And while attempting to bring home the meaning of this verse, Ismail Raji al-Faruqi significantly observes:

If the term 'know' is taken figuratively, then the *Quran* would be telling us that gender and ethnic characteristics were created by God to the end of humans finding in them mutual complementarity and cooperation. All humans are therefore one and the same: the base and ground of Islam's universalism. All humans are one in God's eye except as their deeds distinguish them in moral virtue, in cultural or civilisational achievement. If these deeds are dependent upon preemptive cultural characteristics hampering such achievements, it is a moral duty to alter those characteristics and to grow others, which is always possible. The door to such alterations is never closed. On the other hand, where judgement does take place on the basis of immutable characteristics, a moral crime, namely ethnocentrism is committed. The implications of such a crime are ominous; the unity of humanity is violated, and divine unity is violated as well...[16]

But then the question remains whether the plan for the "Islamization of Knowledge" is valid, or relevant to the noble purpose of creating *ummatic* consciousness. My answer is not in the affirmative in the context of the *Quran's* resounding emphasis that "all knowledge is with Allah".[17] An attempt at Islamising knowledge, therefore, appears to me as Islamisation of Islam. Although we have discussed earlier that Islam is not an ideology related to a particular period in history, yet attempts to confine it within the narrow limits of geopolitical situations continue unabated.

What Allah requires of believers is not an ideologically conscious struggle for establishing a *khilafa* but a consciousness, as His vicegerents, of being able to perceive, understand, feel, experience, affirm, radiate, and communicate the totality of His knowledge in the harmonious depths of the unity of their faith and practice. Allah alone is not only Aware *(Khabir)* but also the knower of what is known and unknown. To Him alone belongs the sovereignty of the Worlds. In the context of the *Quran* sovereignty has deeper implications and dimensions than the ordinary meaning of the term in the Western political sense. While in the Quranic sense no human can claim knowledge of what is known to Allah alone, likewise, conferment of political power in the world on nations and groups, notwithstanding their beliefs, is an integral component of the spiritio-historical process. Being Mighty and Wise in all spheres of His Infinity, the Author of the *Quran* not only lays an undisputed claim to His Omnipotence and Omnipresence but urges us to see that the end of learning is to know Him through observation of the natural phenomena:

> And if all trees in the earth were pens, and the sea, with all seas to help it were ink, the words of Allah could not be exhausted.[18]

While Allah alone is infinitely aware of our actions, our knowledge of ourselves in our relation to the cosmos does not correspond to His encompassing knowledge. Thus our own ignorance compels us to learn that history, mathematics, experimental science, philosophy and various other branches of knowledge consist of highly probable generalisations, not indubitable certainties. In fact, the concept of knowledge, as embedded in the *Quran,* makes itself intelligible to us particularly with reference to the very nature of the whole and its parts. Isn't the whole, being a relatively complete entity, always greater than any of its parts? There is little doubt then that all branches of knowledge are pre-eminently Islamic and cannot be otherwise. Or, more appropriately, they cannot be purely religious or secular or scientific. From the standpoint of the *Quran,* knowledge is all-pervading and all-embracing. The Creator can by no stretch of the imagination be unaware of the prurience of his depraved creatures and their widespread moral corruption on this planet. In fact, both noble and ignoble thoughts which are part of our daily experience call for constant examination for making our knowledge integrated and self-disciplined. Knowledge must therefore control the motives of its seekers and guide their thought and behaviour in harnessing rather than polluting environment.

The approach of the *Quran* is scientific in respect of its repeated emphasis on the need for an incessant struggle throughout history essentially rooted in an enquiry into the spiritual and mundane phenomena in a supernal integral and interactional context of its servant-Lord, seeker-Guide and created-Creator relationship. What Muslim societies need, in the ultimate analysis, is not the "Islamization of Knowledge" but a harmonious relationship between knowledge and human behaviour. And although knowledge is hidden in the Creator's 'signs', yet the question that awaits answer is whether Muslims are prepared to re-orient their quest for knowledge in a spirit of surrender to the Will of Allah and service to mankind. Our understanding of the *Quran* as the source of all knowledge must inflame in us not merely a deeper yearning for knowing the truth in its totality but also a sublime consciousness to practise what we learn in the process of fortifying our belief and faith. The emerging point is that our knowledge, belief and behaviour must converge and merge with the purpose for which Allah created us *vis-a-vis* the cosmic order. The Quranic verse—"And we created not the heavens and the earth, and all that is between them, in play"[19]—assumes profound meaning and significance when we begin to realise that a natural process cannot be fully recognised without recognizing God's ceaseless activity.

Thus while everything in the universe acts in a natural process or, in other words, surrenders to the Will of Allah, man is the only creature granted the "freedom" to obey or flout the natural laws of his natural religion. The point is that each individual and each society or nation have to recognise the vital difference between surrender to the Will of Allah and a futile attempt at creating psychological and social disharmony by following an opposite course. Since human knowledge is by and large a matter of guesswork in the profoundest Quranic context, "a guess cannot take the place of the truth."[20] And considering the belief that "Allah surrounds all things in knowledge,"[21] it is important to bear in mind that Allah enjoins upon us to know the unity of the sun, moon, day, night, firmament and earth in their obedience to the unchangeable laws of nature.[22] And it is against the background of such natural principles of the natural religion that Allah swears: "By the soul, and the proportion and order given to it; and its inspiration as to its wrong and its right;—truly he succeeds that purifies it, and he fails that corrupts it."[23]

Now the only issue in our effort to understand knowledge *vis-a-vis* our belief and behaviour is whether a human soul is ready to follow his nature or debase it. And following nature means following the Straight Path in a spirit of genuine search for our conscience. Isn't a disciplined conscience the most valuable of all possessions to both an individual and a nation? Isn't one's clean and sensitive conscience one's best educator and monitor? In the Quranic sense, ignorance parades as knowledge if the soul of a nation continues to remain steeped in *ammara*. Unless the *umma* endeavours to search its collective conscience in the context of *nafs-i-lawwama*, the nobler intentions underlying the rapid drive for "Islamization of knowledge" will lead it nowhere.

Notes and References

1. Ismail Raji al-Faruqi, *Islamization of Knowledge,* published by International Institute of Islamic Thought (2nd ed. Indian reprint 1988), See Preface.
2. Ibid.
3. Ibid., pp. 38-39.
4. Ibid. p. 32.
5. Ibid.
6. Ibid. p.2.
8. Ibid.
9. It is unfortunate that a scholar of Ismail Raji-al-Faruqi's calibre dubs Muslim nationalist leaders as hypocrites *(munafiqs)* and heretics *(zindiqs).* Ibid. p. 36. While Faruqi raises a legitimate protest against ethnocentrism being the marked characteristic of the nationalism of Westerners, Jews and Russians, it would, however, be a grave historical error to make Muslim nationalist leaders the butt of ridicule and criticism on that ground. What needs to be stressed is that nationalism in the Muslim world is not marked by exclusiveness of individual nationalities or ethnocentrism, but intrinsically, by the manifestation of a spirit of revolt by oppressed people against imperialism. Being a definite stage of the liberation movements, nationalism has a general democratic content for the furtherance of political and economic objectives. Not the least, nationalism is a movement, based upon the folk idioms, history, aspirations, etc., of suppressed nations. Nationalism thus emerges as an ideology of societies entrenched in the quagmire of

colonialism. So deep-rooted has been the legacy of colonialism on the Muslim mind, that both Muslim nationalists and Islamic ideologists continue to serve the interests of their one-time masters by becoming votaries of both Western values and perpetrators and victims of the technological violence of the West respectively.

10. *Quran,* 29/20.
11. Ibid., 22/46.
12. Ibid., Allama Yusuf Ali's tr. note 2825.
13. Ibid. m 29/19.
14. Ibid. m 2/219-20, 164; 3/190; 6/95/99; 17/12; 10/5-6; 30/20-27; 45/3-6; 36/37-40; 41/53 etc.
15. Ibid., 49/13.
16. Ismail Raji al-Faruqi, op. cit., 34-35.
17. *Quran,* 46/23.
18. Ibid., 31/27; 18/109.
19. Ibid., 44/38; 38/27.
20. Ibid., 53/28.
21. Ibid., 65/12.
22. Ibid., 91/1-6.
23. Ibid., 91/7-9.

8

SELF-REALISATION IN THE CONTEMPORARY WORLD

One of the ninety-nine special names of Allah, occurring frequently in the *Quran*, is *al-Basir*—"The All-Seeing One".[1] Our actions, always watched by Allah, are either intentional or unintentional, habitual or spontaneous, emotional or unemotional, inspired or uninspired, individual or collective, and above all, thoughtful or thoughtless. As the pride of creation, our actions can by no means go unnoticed in the continuing creative process characterising the cosmos. And if Allah is with the man wheresoever he may be how can his activities escape His all-pervading notice?[2] In fact, Allah is "nearer to him than (his) jugular vein."[3] Only a few people realise this Truth and so they constantly strive to live in His presence. Such people are true believers, distinguishable from the general lot of believers.

True believers ceaselessly and consciously endeavour to be as steadfast in their faith and actions as the *Quran* urges them to be. To be a true believer always demands an earnest desire to know the Creator through self-introspection. The simple but significant questions that always strike his mind are: "Where do I come from?" "What is or should be my mission on this planet?" "Where am I going?" These questions are intrinsically of spiritual import since they occur in our minds amidst the welter of the worldly facts. They are, therefore, likely to broaden an objective understanding of the phenomena called the cosmos. The questions of metaphysical nature cease to be speculative once we begin to realise the nature of existence, truth and knowledge in our own actions.

The *Quran* grants us freedom of the highest degree for choosing the Straight Path or the one that may lead one astray. While harmony and peace epitomise the Straight Path, discord and violence characterise the other way. Man can be either peace-loving or a trouble maker. Allah did not send him to this planet for fomenting trouble and shedding blood but for stabilising his inner self and the world through self-discovery and intellectual understanding. For this reason alone *din* was designated Peace (Islam). The meaning and purpose of *din* is best exemplified in the behavioural norms of Muslims. Whenever they see each other, return to the world after concluding the regular daily prayers *(salat)*, enter their homes after the routine work, pass by the graveyards, and enter into correspondence with each other, the only word they utter is 'peace'. Still greater, the *Quran* exhorts the believer to say peace when confronted with an ignorant person.[4] But the resonant words of peace pouring forth from the mouth of a believer may sound superficial to many, for it is he who has been accused of disturbing peace in most parts of the world. Is there any dichotomy in the behaviour of Muslims or is there any contradiction in the basic Islamic concept of peace?

Being essentially a religion of peace, Islam has a centuries old history of the tradition of peaceful transition of the societies exposed to its radiant influence. The relative inner stability of the souls of a considerable number of people assimilated in Islam either out of conviction or through a process of acculturation during centuries of orderly evolution can be explained in spiritual and historical terms respectively. However, what needs not to be ignored is the persistent dark and disturbing legacy of colonialism. Didn't colonialism inject a long-persisting poison into the psyche of Muslims? Unless we realise the dynamics of Muslim politics in terms of their constant preoccupation with the cankerous legacies of colonialism[5], it would be difficult for us to understand the import of Peace that symbolises Islam.

Notwithstanding the historical nature of violence that characterises certain Muslim societies, Muslim leadership, nevertheless, needs to think in terms of solving their genuine problems as a matter of long-term rather than short-term short-sighted measures. The need for struggle is the quintessence of Islam. But the spirit of struggle needs to be nourished or baked in a spiritio-historical rather than a purely historical mould. Neither will the rights of people be vindicated through carrying on a militant struggle, nor will they continue to be repressed for all time to come through a brutal display of force by the State power.

The present turmoil in the Valley of Kashmir, for instance, has not arisen all of a sudden but is the logical culmination of the reckless belief in the efficacy of the gun as against belief in the Quranic saying: "Allah does not change the condition of any nation unless it strives in that direction".[6]

Change, in the Quranic sense, has deep-rooted implications for the future of a nation. It should not be understood as a mere mechanical recitation of a formula, but as elevation or ascension, an absorption of consciousness in a determined will to transcend the baser self or instincts. When, to use the phraseology of Toynbee, a "creative minority" under the leadership of a "creative personality" is capable of self-denial of the Prophetic type, it may set in motion a phenomenon, called *jihad bin nafs*[7] or the greater *jihad (jihad-i akbar)*[8]. Such a phenomenon is of profound significance in the context of the *Quran* and, also, in view of the continued relevance of the *Sunna*. The facts related to this continued, patient and determined struggle show the reality of certain deepest relations, of still unknown nature to social scientists, between man and God. While Muslim leaders in the contemporary scene are seldom conscious of the objective importance of the spiritio-historical relationship, yet they have almost always neglected it under the rattling influence, power and lethality of the imported weapon. How long can Muslims afford to ignore the *Sunna*? How long should they act without thought? Muslims cannot learn to distinguish right from wrong[9] in a state of cultivated ignorance typical of the mentality of the mob. The activities of the Quranic consciousness thus demand not the group affiliations of a political or ideological nature but sublime consciousness of a higher degree that determines, in an orderly and evolutionary manner, the number, the quality, and the intensity of the manifestations of individual consciousness. This will enable an individual to guard against the tendency of weaning himself from himself. Once responsible Muslim individuals and leaders in their religious and public life realise the value of consciousness we have been advocating, the *umma* will no longer be marked by the atrophy of certain activities of religio-political consciousness. Isn't pursuit of scientific, technological and intellectual research possible within the parameters of our consciousness? Isn't such a struggle, in the context of the *Quran*, necessary for creating an environment in which a balance of competitive co-existence rather than terror forms the aim of our efforts?

Muslims need to ponder on the *Quran* in a spirit of both self-discovery, self-reform and scientific enquiry. "Who so chooseth Satan for a patron instead of Allah is verily a loser and his loss is manifest. He promiseth them and stirreth up desires in them, and Satan promiseth them only to beguile."[10] Didn't the Arabs' sole dependence on the Soviet military technology bring about their humiliating defeat in 1967? What did Iraq and Iran gain out of their conflict? Did it not benefit the developed nations as suppliers of arms? How did Saddam's arrogance coupled with his sole reliance on Soviet arms benefit the Iraqi nation? South Asia has also to tell its story of sorrows. Did the arms supplied to Pakistan by the United States work wonders in the Indo-Pakistan wars fought over Kashmir? Muslim enthusiasts have now begun to pin high hopes on the F-16 rather than on the inbuilt hope of true believers in receiving Allah's help through constant struggle. That Muslims have somehow or the other reinforced the image of America as their deliverer during periods of acute crisis is also attested to by their vain hope during the Indo-Pakistan war in 1971 that the US Seventh Fleet might come to the help of Pakistan. These simple facts have been intriguing the minds of sensitive Muslims notwithstanding the ruthless pace at which they are forgotten in occasional occurrence of euphoric events. However, they cannot be brushed aside in a searching enquiry after self-discovery.

Since I do not have the credentials of a spiritual leader, it would be foolish on my part to describe America as "The Great Satan". But the objective truth which I cannot suppress in the context of the Quranic dictum—"Don't confound truth with untruth knowingly"[11]—is that Muslim leadership is least thoughtful about its cynicism on the one hand and simultaneously its congenital dependence on the strength of "enemy-manufactured" weapons. Hasn't this phenomenon robbed Peter to pay Paul? Hasn't the wild race for acquiring sophisticated weapons roused passions and expectations of Muslims to the fever pitch without invigorating their inner faith or inner conscience? Doesn't this situation question the faith of Muslims in the Omnipotence and Omnipresence of Allah? Where is the intellect of the Muslim 'think tank' so highly praised in the

Quran? How long will or should Muslims allow themselves to be duped by the Machiavellian diplomacy of pitting one nation against another? Should Muslims continue to allow themselves to take a lethal dose of this poisonous imported mixture?

The valiant struggle of the Afghans against the Soviet Union had, however, different dimensions. They had no alternative but to resist the Soviet forces for several reasons. Both in the context of the *Quran* and in terms of the Communist ideology the aggressor (Soviet Union) was the living example of the greatest anti-God activist on this planet. America's role in promoting the spirit of *jihad* among Afghans and Muslim enthusiasts elsewhere against the Communist invader needs to be understood from a deeper perspective of greater purpose of Allah in uniting the 'People of the Book' *(ahl-i-Kitab)* against unbelief. For this reason, also, Islamic disciplines have flourished in Western universities, notwithstanding academic criticism of their politically motivated research. True, America also supported the Mujahideen in order to promote its ideological interests, but it must be admitted that without the help of America (also Pakistan) the Afghans would not have been able to carry their struggle to successful fruition within a relatively short period in historical terms.

The resulting Soviet discomfiture had far-reaching implications for the Muslim world in particular and the world in general. Besides proving to be an important factor in the disintegration of the Soviet Union, America now began liking to play God. One doubts whether Washington would have attacked Baathist Iraq had not the dismemberment of Soviet Union destroyed the concept of balance of power. Whatever may be one's thinking on one of the 'ifs' of contemporary history, the irony remains that the Sa'udi permission to America and its allies to use the 'holy land' as a base for its military operations against Iraq served to bolster up the somewhat Big Brother image of America controlling every aspect of Muslim countries while pretending to be friendly and kindly. America's subsequent efforts, in the wake of its intervention over Kuwait, in the direction of creating a new world order are therefore worthy of some reflection.

The American vision of the emerging new world order is primarily based on its vested interest, seeking a world structure that retains its pre-eminence. This vision has been centred on the state and, therefore, on its locus. Notwithstanding seemingly good intentions underlying the desired goal, all efforts in that direction are bound to come to naught if the American and its Western allies do not realise that the major threat to the world peace is the instability of its own making that characterises some sensitive regions of the Muslim world. This situation has been the unfortunate result of Western colonial conspiracy aimed at keeping Muslim nations vulnerable in both political and economic terms. However, two challenging issues—Palestine and Kashmir—once solved, would enable Muslims to work as co-partners in a process at the global level on the Quranic principles of co-existence. The Arafat-Rabin Accord, though flawed, has nevertheless shown the futility of carrying on an incessant armed struggle in the context of a manufactured obsession with military preparations for all possible contingencies.

The current unipolarity of the world seems to me a temporary phase through which Muslims must need to steer carefully rather than in thoughtless haste. Aren't most Muslim nations weaker in their dependence on the West for economic or military aid? Don't they have many vulnerabilities—systemic and political? In such a situation, fear of the Muslim bloc or the Muslim world emerging as challenge to the West or its envisioned new world order is baseless.

Even if Muslims emerge as power in the very remote future, they would not be in a position to subjugate the West militarily. History tells us that the Muslim military adventure on the Western soil, notwithstanding the excellent standard that culture and science achieved in Spain, ultimately proved to be a nightmare. The point seldom stressed is that political power in Moorish Spain did not produce spiritual eminence. Islam in Spain remained a political rather than a socio-religious phenomenon. Sufism appeared in Spain much later than it did in the East. Until the conquest of Spain in 711 Islam had not reached there as a spiritual force. And despite the Spanish ancestry of one of the greatest Sufis, Ibn al-Arabi (d. 1240), the Sufi presence in Spain was by no means remarkable. For political reasons, Islam in Spain did not emerge as a spiritio-social force. From the standpoint of the history of Sufism, it must be stressed that Sufism in Spain was a decidedly religio-political, rather a "social" phenomenon. Richard Bulliet remarks: "Factions composed of the descendants of earlier converts tended to eschew Sufism while descendants of later converts were more likely to favour it".[12] Still more, the noted scholar adds a footnote: "The revolt in western Spain led by the Sufi Ibn Qasi from 1142 to 1151 shows the political potential of Sufism....."[13] The point that emerges is that Islam in Spain, essentially centred on an aristocracy among indigenous converts, could not create cultural institutions of its own like *khanqahs* through which it could filter down the social ladder. This explains to a large extent why in the early centuries of Islamic civilisation greater parts of Arab and Ajam functioned more as the recipients and centres of religio-cultural institutional forms—*madrasas, khanqahs*, Sufi brotherhoods and so on. It is an irony of Islamic history that while the mosques of Spain have since remained nothing more than haunting momentoes of architectural excellence and spiritual decadence of the Spanish Muslim patrician class, the *khanqahs* of the East (particularly in South Asia) in their pristine simplicity have continued to remain impregnable fortresses against the acculturative onslaughts of every kind other than Islamic.

Viewed in the context of the Quranic emphasis that sovereignty of the world belongs to Allah alone,[14] conferment of partial regional sovereignty in the cosmic order on personifications of the Devil or unbelief is not more than a contra-indication for the souls who do not waste their life in covetting such an honour. Superbly conscious of this reality, the best of the enlightened souls among the *ulama-i-Haqq* and Sufis were never lured by the worldly politics. The fact that they did not even accept offers to serve the caliphs and the sultans in highest official positions proves the point (e.g., Imam Abu Hanifa, Imam Ahmad bin Hanbal and scores of other Muslim scholars and Sufis).

"Allah grants sovereignty to whom He will."[15] Behind such verses in the *Quran* is the divine wisdom to distinguish right from wrong while testing the moral and spiritual strength of a true believer. Didn't Allah grant sovereignty to the Pharaoh? Doesn't He grant power to whom He will and doesn't He withhold power from whom He will?[16] Had it been the purpose of Allah to grant complete and unlimited sovereignty of the world to true believers alone He would have done so ever since the creation of this world. Contrariwise, the unified concept underlying the spirit of the Grace bestowed on true believers is the Grace bestowed upon them from His Presence *(Ladunna)*[17]. The Semitic Prophets, particularly Moses, Christ and Muhammad, were vouchsafed Grace rather than power in the modern political sense. And it is worthwhile to reflect on the prayer that the Prophet was taught to recite on the eve of his entry into Medina:

> And say: My Lord: Cause me to come in with a firm incoming and to go out with a firm outgoing; And give me from Thy Presence a sustaining power.[18]

The mission of the Prophet Muhammad was neither exclusively religious nor political; it was spiritio-historical with several ramifications for the religio-political development of the *umma* on *Tawhidic Weltanschuung*. However it has been the conventional wisdom of the West to study Islam from a distance through the binoculars of its triumphant reason. Thus writes Arnold Toynbee, "the public career of the Prophet Muhammad falls into two sharply distinct and seemingly contradictory chapters."[19] The basis of this argument is a partial understanding of the role of the Prophet without an iota of understanding or even knowledge of the historical significance of the *mi'raj*. We have already hinted at the scholarly attempts at highlighting the *Hijra* rather than the *mi'raj*. While the *mi'raj* and *Hijra* are inseparable parts of the totality called the *Sunna*, nevertheless, Toynbee expatiates on "two sharply distinct and seemingly contradictory chapters"[20] of the Prophet's personality. As he observes: "In the first he is occupied in preaching a religious revelation by methods of pacific evangelisation; in the second he is occupied in building up a political and military power and in using this power in the very way which, in other cases, has turned out disastrous for a religion that takes to it. In this Medinese chapter Muhammad used his new-found material power for the purpose of enforcing conformity with, at any rate, the outward observances of the religion which he had founded in the previous chapter of his career, before his momentous withdrawal from Mecca to Medina. On this showing the *Hijrah* ought to mark the date of the ruin of Islam and not the date since consecrated as that of its foundation. How are we to explain the hard fact that a religion which was launched on the world as the militant faith of a barbarian war-band should have succeeded in becoming a universal church, in spite of having started under a spiritual handicap that might have been expected, on all analogies, to prove prohibitive?"[21]

The terms in which Toynbee understands the "public career" of the Prophet Muhammad are neither objectively spiritual nor historical, but Western. The paradigm of "Mecca" and "Medina", first introduced by Edward Gibbon in his *magnum opus*,[22] is characteristic of the Western mind's tendency to exclusively define Islam in terms other than Islamic. The *Quran* nowhere invests the Prophet with a divine mission or authority of conquering the world with the sole aim of political aggrandizement. The ultimate concept of the triumph of *din* over unbelief, in fact, emerges in the Quran as a manifestation of Allah's Will for the historical fruition of the primordial *din* under the supernal leadership of Muhammad.

> And (as for the believers) hath attuned their hearts. If thou (Muhammad) hadst spent all that is in the earth thou could not have attuned their hearts, but Allah had attuned them. Lo He is Mighty.[23]

This verse has significantly the context of Medina. Contrary to Toynbee's conception of Islam as a "militant faith" under the "political leadership" of its "founder" we need to understand the role of the last of the Prophets in a broader Quranic perspective of the triumph of *Tawhidic* universalism over the forces of ethnocentrism. Again, in the context of the following verse, probably revealed about the time of the Battle of the Ditch *(Khandaq)*, also called the Battle of the Confederates *(Ahzab)*, "We can imagine the comfort it (the verse) gave to the Muslims who were besieged in Medina by a force ten times their number."[24]

"Allah hath promised such of you as believe and do good works that He will surely make them to succeed (the present rulers) in the earth as He caused those who were before them to succeed (others); and that He will surely establish for them their religion which He hath approved for them in exchange safely after their fear. They serve Me. They ascribe nothing as partner unto Me. Those who disbelieve henceforth, they are the miscreants."[25] The preceding verses of the same *surah* that "the messenger hath no other charge than to convey (the message), plainly",[26] will be fully understood in relation to the two verses[27] (24/56-57) following the verse[28] that may be read out of context by the protagonists of the so-called "militant" or "political" Islam. "Establish worship and pay the poor their due and obey the messenger, that haply you may find mercy. Think not that the disbelievers can escape in the land. Fire will be their home—a hapless journey's end."[29]

The fact is that the *Quran* guides human consciousness not through a labyrinth of mental controversies but through integration of all disciplines of the mind with religious duties, morals, social and economic policy as well as with legal practice.

Paradoxically, however, contemporary Muslim perceptions of the role of Muhammad are as misplaced as those of the Western mind. In fact the understanding process itself is derailed not only by the legacies of apologetic historiography, Orientalism, colonialism, imperialism but also in no small measure blinkered by some sort of ideological ethnocentrism not borne out by the *Quran*. Thus the ideology of "Islamization" in the political sense is not more than an attempt to define Islam in terms of territorially-characterised state or state religion rather than in the context of *Quran's* universal spiritual ethics. This is the reason that the modern Islamic state is hardly capable of providing either spiritual or intellectual leadership to the *umma*. The "Islamic Revolution" of Iran particularly illustrates the point.

Ayatollah Khomeini, not unlike Maulana Maududi of the *Jamat-i-Islami* and Hasan al-Banna of the Muslim Brotherhood, had a view of the world that drew a sharp contrast between East and West.[30] This view of the world was rooted in his hatred of the West, bred by colonialism and imperialism: "The foul claws of imperialism have clutched at the heart of the lands of the people of the *Quran,* with our national wealth and resources being devoured by imperialism...with the poisonous culture of imperialism penetrating out to the depth of towns and villages throughout the Muslim world, displacing the culture of the *Quran.*"[31] The immediate impact of the Iranian Revolution on the 'Muslim World' was therefore the import of inspirational fervour into the societies undergoing the process of Westernisation. The holy war or *jihad* against all that was "un-Islamic" became the credo of Islamic revolutionary movements. The commitment to Islam in terms of spreading its message and promoting its cause was a primary foreign policy objective enshrined in the constitution of the Islamic Republic of Iran, "to perpetuate the revolution both at home and abroad."[32]

Whatever the significance of the global impact of the Iranian Revolution, its historical character stimulated thinking more and more on religio-politico rather than spiritio-historical grounds. Little wonder that the mob mobilisation of militant fervour for the "defence" of Islam has since remained the distinctive characteristic of the "Islamic Revolution" of Iran. Thus commitment to Islam has been marked by ideological euphoria rather than by the act of pledging oneself to Islam in a strict spiritio-historical sense. Although Khomeini stood for the spread of Islam through peaceful means, yet the adherents of "Islamic ideology" have shunned that approach in preference to confrontation and armed struggle. "We want Islam to spread everywhere but this does not mean that we intend to export it by the bayonet... If the governments submit and behave in accordance with Islamic tenets, support them, if not, fight them without fear of anyone."[33]

From the standpoint of the Quran and *Sunna*, an attempt to impose rather than experience Islam gives birth to several questions: Is it Islam to impose Islam from above? Is it the primary objective of "Islamic Revolution" or Islam to use Islam as the most effective means of political mobilisation? Is it Islam or "Islamic ideology" that is at the root of the Muslim diaspora?

It must be stressed that the legacy of the inherited technology of power and historical violence from the West has seldom allowed modern Muslim leadership to grow and mould into the Quranic model of a universality. The "culture of the *Quran*" can surely prove an effective antidote to a barrage of views on Islam provided its creative ability to communicate in dialogue with other cultures, primarily at the individual level, is not further allowed to be superseded by the national or religio-political exigencies of Muslim states. Should Muslims realise the necessity of a change from within for the long-term objectives of Islam, they will automatically cease to dissipate their strength by resorting to the historical violence of overthrowing "un-Islamic" governments with the avowed aim of establishing an "Islamic state". True, in the context of the *Quran*, people have the right to overthrow an unjust ruler or system; but the intrinsic point that is seldom stressed is whether the *Quran* provokes mechanisms of *coup de main* or *coup detat* or mob violence under a charismatic leadership or galvanises an impassioned and sustained social response inspired by the 'model' and the 'ideal'.

Change is the essence of the Quranic historical thought. "Allah does not change the condition of any nation unless it strives in that direction."[34] The Quranic concept of change is not related to mere outward form but a deep-felt change within individual souls. So let us try to seek answers to some of our basic questions. Can religio-political ideology allow human personality to grow and mould into the Quranic model of universality? Can Allah be our Protecting Friend in our seemingly Islamic but essentially ineluctable domestic and factional politicking?[35] What are the preconditions for change in the life of individuals and nations?

Notwithstanding the transcendence of Allah, the *Quran* also emphasizes the immanence (in-dwelling of the universe, time etc.[36]) underlying His concept. When we surrender to Allah, we actually affirm our faith in both His transcendence and immanence. And Allah is the one Who cannot be seen but simultaneously His presence can be felt on realising that He is always watching us.[37] In such a context, our position is not more than that of His servants. He is our Lord and we are His servants. This kind of relationship is a matter of faith and not more than that. But when a believer has the ability to recognise the immanence of Allah, he rises above the average believer whose actions are more or less mechanistic in a given relationship of mere obedience to the injunctions of the Transcendent. A true believer, however, endeavours to see beyond the mechanism of obedience in the *Shari'a*-structured relationship in his own thought and behaviour. Such a relationship is incapable of being readily grasped by the ordinary mind; hence deep thinking on the *Quran* and moulding one's actions in accordance with the evolutionary processes of one's understanding of the Book are the *sine qua non* for the inner stability of our souls, mind and the society we live in. In such a process, a believer proves himself to be the stable embodiment of the *Shari'a* in the world and, in fact, Allah becomes his Protecting Friend towards the fruition of a supreme goal, i.e., peace within ourselves, peace with neighbours and peace the world over, *Pax Islamica*. Allah created the world with wisdom. He made Islam the source of peace in the trouble-torn world.

From the standpoint of Semitic religions, it can be argued that at the root of Adam's descent into this world were the

Devil's acts of defiance and deception. The Devil disobeyed God, thereby causing Adam and Eve to commit an act of disobedience through fraud. The concept of the Devil has been derided by rationalists; for non-believers it is as impalable as the concept of God, considering the supernatural phenomena embodying the very basis of religion. However, for such reasoning minds we would equate Allah with the forces of love, peace and stability and the Devil with hate, disharmony and violence in the world. Allah does not represent merely power but also love. And He loves those who strive in His Way. Who are such people? We will attempt to study the *Quran* from cover to cover in an effort to understand Allah's concept of His true servants.

Who are believers in the context of the *Quran*?

"They are who believe in

1) the one Universal God,
2) the Message that came through Muhammad and the Signs *(ayat)* as interpreted on the basis of personal responsibility,
3) the Message delivered by other Teachers in the past.
    These are mentioned in three groups:
1) Abraham Ismail, Isaac, Jaccob, and the Tribes: Of these Abraham had apparently a Book (IXXXVII, 19) and the others followed this tradition;
2) Moses and Jesus, who each left a scripture: these scriptures are still extant, though not in their pristine form; and
3) Other scriptures, Prophets, or Messengers of Allah, not specifically mentioned in the *Quran* (11/78)."[38]

The believers make no difference "between one and another" of the prophets.[39] The Message of all prophets (in the essentials) was one and forms the cardinal teaching of Islam. One who believes in such terms surrenders to Allah and is therefore on the right path. The indivisible Message of Allah is universal and those who corrupt it create a division or schism.[40] The deviators are the Jews who, though they preached Unity, followed false gods, and the Christians who invented the Trinity or "borrowed it from paganism". The seekers after the Truth are therefore warned against those who corrupted the universal Truth: "They say: Become Jews or Christians if you would be guided (to salvation). Say thou: 'Nay' (I would rather) the Religion of

Abraham the True, And he joined not gods with Allah."[41] Against this background, it would be worthwhile to make the following verse the basis of our growing spiritual and historical consciousness. "(Our religion) Takes its hue from Allah, and who can give a better hue than Allah. It is He, whom we worship."[42]

Sibgath: The root-meaning implies a dye or colour. It is a substance used for giving colour to paper, cloth, hair, etc. While the language of the *Quran* is rich in similitudes, the metaphor of the divine colour is revealing in several respects. First, it distinguishes the role of a true servant of Allah from several believers. The similitude of hue assigns a special role to His servants in the variegated structures of His own creation.

It follows that the Quranic concept of the universe is both monistical and pluralistic. In the former sense, there is only one basic substance or principle as the ground of Reality. But, as a matter of objective fact, Reality is comprehensible or recognisable in the pluralistic work of His own making. Contrary to the Western sociological and philosophical concepts of monism and pluralism, the *Quran* exhorts us to recognise the deeper truth underlying both the unity and multiplicity of His created universe. From the standpoint of the *Quran*, the universe is neither the result of a current of accidental events nor that of an evolutionary process. The centre of gravity in the *Quran* is man in relation to his Creator and Nourisher. Man is made of both matter and spirit. Matter and spirit, though seemingly at odds with each other, are not opposites in the Quranic sense. Nor do they coincide in the monadical sense of a spiritualised matter. The finite and the infinite are not opposites but an indivisible unity that is spatially and physically individuated. Both form the greater part of the Unity called the Infinite. True that the spirit belongs to the Infinite and invisible world, but the moment the matter begins to interact with the Infinite in a spirit of self-realisation, the notional barriers between matter and spirit start disappearing. Consequently, the spirit of the human body, intrinsically endowed with the ability of clear perception, attains the rationality of the highest degree as distinct from what the ordinary rationality of the mind cannot perceive. The rational soul of man contains infinity in itself in contrast to the finite mind of man beyond the point set by its reason. And while mind and matter produce ideologies and institutions as a result of interactions, so do interaction of mind, soul and body produce a model of excellence in the form of human personality. This change in the individuality of man takes place under the nourishing care of Allah's Infinity.

The concept of change within the framework of the *Quran* is thus related to the human response to the basic Quranic premise that Allah is the final Cause of causes. The main task is, therefore, not to seek the radical transformation of the society or the world but a gradual adaptation of human souls to spiritual ethics through self-discovery. It is not so much the idea of conquering the world as that of harnessing it through self-realisation that embodies the spiritio-social structure of the *Quran*. The essence of Allah's exhortations to His servants is recognition of the personality as the primary reality and the supreme spiritual value, the personality being regarded as the spiritual primary element of His whole creation.

The personality of the man of God is, therefore, colourful in the sense of being cast in the mould of the natural colour *(Sibgath ullah)*. The entire period of his life has a colour of its own. His thinking is not colourless, nor are his actions. He is part and parcel of his society and its history, yet his style of inner and social life is full of brightness. What imparts special colour to his spiritual manhood is the lifelong effort for seeking the countenance *(ridha)* of Allah. This struggle is not part of his mere self but that of the soul, mind and body in close interaction with the society of which he is an essential part. The key term for such a gifted soul is the protege of Allah *(wali)*. In fact, the term is derivative of two comprehensive terms Friend *(Wali)* and Lover *(Muhib)* with which Allah repeatedly defines His special relations with His servants. The concept of personality that emerges in the *Quran* is the condescension of divinity, and the exaltation of humanity. The nature of its existence is not mysterious but objective. The Quranic personality is the one that stands at the absolute centre of humanity. In Sufic terms, he is the pole *(Qutb)*. He is the living proof of the Absolute and Perfect Truth, the highest that humanity can reach. In the following chapter we will attempt to discover the personality through the vocabulary of the *Quran*.

Notes and References

1. *Quran*, 40/56; 42/27; 57/4 etc.
2. Ibid., 57/4.
3. Ibid., 50/16; also 56/85.
4. Ibid., 25/63.
5. See the author's letter in *The Times of India*, 16 June, 1994.
6. *Quran*, 13/11; 8/53.
7. A tradition makes the Prophet rank the "greater endeavour or greater warfare" (*jihad-i akbar*) above the "lesser warfare" (*jihad-i asghar*, i.e., the war against disbelief), and explain the "greater warfare" as meaning "earnest striving within the soul" (*mujahadat al-nafs*). See Sayyid Ali Hujwiri, *Kashaf al-Mahjub*, tr. Nicholson, p.200.
8. *Quran*, 25/52. The greater endeavour or greater warfare, also called *jihad-i kabira*, is waged with the force of Allah's revelation. True, the verse has Meccan context; but this kind of endeavour (*jihad bil Quran*) has eternal significance and relevance to our roles as individuals in constituting the *umma* on its pristine foundations. "Say: truly, my prayer and my service of sacrifice, my life and death, are (all) for Allah, the Cherisher of the worlds," Ibid., 6/162. "And that they strive earnestly in our cause, them, We surely guide upon our paths." Ibid., 29/69. The eternal mission of inviting people to universal good rather than launching a struggle for attaining worldly power is the epitome of the Quranic message. If this were not the purpose of the *Quran*, there would have been neither Pharaoh nor Nimrod symbolising ignominy in the manifestation of their sovereignty as against Abraham and Moses representing divine grace and power as vicegerents. The invocations of the prayers of Abraham, Moses and several other prophets, mentioned in the *Quran*, in the daily religious obligations of Muslims must serve as eye-openers for those who unduly stress the importance of political power (*daula*) for enforcing the laws of Islam. From the Quranic standpoint, the bulk of the people of the Book (*Ahl-i Kitab*) seldom reflect on these invocatory prayers for harmonising their personal and social behaviour.
9. Ibid., 3/104.
10. Ibid., 4/119-20.
11. Ibid., 2/42.
12. Richard Bulliet, *Conversion to Islam*, Oxford University Press, p. 126.
13. Ibid., p.153 n.
14. *Quran*, 3/26; 9/113; 42/53; 2/284 etc.
15. The Quranic concept of sovereignty needs to be understood in the spiritio-historical rather than religio-political context in which sense

it vests neither with the people nor with an absolute ruler. While despotism dies with wielders of power and absolute authority, the outward grandeur of great empires and even small kingdoms, vanishes in thin air in the twinkling of an eye in the Quranic time sense. Although the essence of democracy is in accord with the spirit of the *Quran* for putting an end to exploitation of every kind, yet no democratic government can claim itself to be egalitarian or benevolent in nature. As a matter of fact, imperialist forces have often masqueraded as champions of democracy and liberal values. The *Quran*, on the other hand, is explicit on the question of principles of government. Allah is the Absolute Ruler *(Ahkam al-Hakimin)*. He grants licence to rule a certain part of the globe to whom He wills. The recipients of such power are both rulers or nations and religious leaders. While in the case of the former power is a trust as well as a trial for managing the worldly affairs in accordance with the universal ethics of primordial *din*, in the latter case sovereignty symbolises the power bestowed on the chosen few from Allah's Presence *(ladunna)*; and whose mission as Prophets, *Ulama-i Haqq* and Sufis is to wage an incessant struggle for the enforcement of the moral code *(Shari'a)* through precept and example. The Quranic verse, referring to the Prophet Yusuf, "Thou has given (something) of sovereignty and has taught me (something) of the interpretation of events" (Ibid., 12/101) thus needs to be understood in a deeper spiritio-historical sense.

16. *Quran.*
17. Ibid., 18/65.
18. Ibid., 17/80.
19. Arnold Toynbee, *A Study of History*, abridged ed., Vol., I New York, London, 1965, p. 55
20. Ibid.
21. Ibid., pp. 555-56.
22. See Edward Gibbon, *The Rise and Fall of Roman Empire.*
23. *Quran,* 8/63.
24. *The Holy Quran,* tr. Yusuf Ali, 3032 n.
25. Ibid., 24/55.
26. Ibid., 24/54.
27. Ibid., 24/56-57.
28. Ibid., 24/55.
29. Ibid., 24/56-57.
30. "Neither East nor West only Islam" was the slogan of the Iranian Revolution. However, "neither of the East nor of the West" *(la sharqiyya-tin la garabiyya-tin)* has deeper spiritual meaning in the Quranic sense (24/35).
31. Quoted in John L. Esposito, *The Islamic Threat: Myth or Reality,* OUP, New York, 1993, p. 109.

32. "Constitution of the Islamic Republic of Iran", *Middle East Journal* 34 (1980): 185 (Quoted in Ibid., p. 114).

33. Quoted in Esposito and Piscatori, "Global Impact," p. 322.

34. *Quran*, 13/11.

35. In spite of their commitment to *jihad* against the common enemy, the Afghan *mujahideen* have shown more loyalty to tribal ideology characterised by factional politics than Islam after their victory over the Soviet forces.

36. "...and know that God stands between a man and his heart and that to Him you shall be mustered." *Quran*, 8/24; see also 50/16. "And in the earth are Signs for those whose faith is sure, and (also) yourselves. See you not?" Ibid., 51/20-21.

37. Islam in Prophetic terms consists in doing everything as gracefully as possible including particularly the daily worship with this belief "as if you were seeing Him, if you do not see Him, He sees you." Bukhari, *Tajrid al-Bukhari*, pp. 27-28.

38. *The Holy Quran*, tr. Yusuf Ali, 135 n. The translator aptly comments: "The heart is the innermost seat of man's affections and desires: but Allah intervenes between man and his heart." 1197 n.

39. Ibid., 2/136.

40. Ibid., 2/136-137.

41. Ibid., 2/135.

42. Ibid., 2/138.

9

THE QURANIC CONCEPT OF PERSONALITY

Two comprehensive terms often repeated by Muslims but least reflected upon are "In the Name of Allah, the Most Beneficent and the Most Merciful" and "Thanks be to the Nourisher of the Worlds". But then the Prophet Muhammad's name also evokes their praise (durud) for the historic fact that he unfolded all that was in humanity. He was the most perfect of the prophets sent before in the sense that his life saw the fruition of their mission. His life was not simply an era in the annals of Arabia but, as a matter of fact, in the history of humankind. His Sunna continues to remind us that the world will be as little as humanity will ever be without him. The epithet 'Grace of the Worlds'[1] used in the Quran for the Prophet is well worth all languages of the world. The only way to vindicate the universality of his message is the need for rekindling the torch of his grace through peaceful efforts. The greatest and the most momentous fact which the Quran records is the fact of the Prophet's all-encompassing grace. All the lines of grace converge upon his humanity. All the great purposes of human existence culminate in him.

The believers in the Quran have been divinely invested with the authority to act. But each action should take its hue from the word of Allah. And every word that the Quran utters about His protege has a meaning related to the serious occupation of His servant's whole existence. The task and triumph of the Quran is not only to sanctify, but more than that, to enlighten, refine and elevate humanity on the highest pedestal of the truth. It is to make individuals, societies and nations just and upright in their dealings. Islam does not emerge in the Quran as a religion of transcendental abstraction, or illuminating speculation or state religion, but as an objective reality exemplified in man's development as a personality. The scope and depth of man's development as an individual are the scope of his assimilation of the social transformation and creation of the social itself. The ultimate triumph of *din* over unbelief under the leadership of Muhammad and consequent emergence and development of Islam as a world civilisation are at the same time historical forms and types of the individual. Allah who is the object of our hopes and of our faith, and the subject of our love is nothing but all-embracing Love Himself (*al-Wudud*)[2]. The point He repeatedly hammers into our minds is about our own cruelty in contrast to His benevolence. The *Quran* has its best exponents not in the heads of "Islamic government"[3] but in the noblest lives of innumerable individuals centred round bringing all law, as well as all conduct, into subjection and conformity to its *Shari'a*. And if the *Quran* has taught anything to mankind, it is that the method of moral, spiritual and intellectual development is intrinsically that of evolution, not that of revolution. The *Quran* is addressed to men of intellect (*ulul al-bab*). Let a believer reflect on the primary importance of evolution before the mob mentality of revolution leads to severe impairment of his intellectual capacity and personality integration. The plight of Muslims in the fast changing world needs to be understood not only in their sense of deprivation, but more importantly, in the impoverishment of their souls and intellect from the strict viewpoint of the *Quran*. This phenomenon rises from an emotional state out of tune with the spiritual and ideational content of evolution. Unless this missing link is restored in the individual souls of Muslims, a euphoric expression of Islam will carry very little weight. While modern Muslim thinkers[4] sought to interpret the *Quran* in ideological terms for combating the forces of Western and Communist imperialism, our endeavour would be in the hope of rediscovering a world communications network in the spiritio-social sphere through the vocabulary of the *Quran*.

Muslims repeatedly thank Allah without exercising their minds or souls. As the *Quran* states: "We have indeed created man in the best of moulds. Then do We abase him (to be the lowest of the low, except such as believe) and do righteous deeds. For they shall have a reward unfailing."[5] Two points are worthy of consideration here. Man's basic nature is purest and best but what makes him fall lower than the beasts in the estimation of

Allah is his propensity to think low. What distinguishes man from the animal species is his ability to think. Thinking in the right direction, or against the Straight Path will mould his behaviour in such a manner that he will become either the embodiment of peace and stability in the world for His cause alone, or its direct opposite. A true understanding of his position in the universe and about Allah's goodness, wisdom and power will constantly keep him aware of the beauty of living in His Presence. But the man whose thinking does not allow him to rise above the narrow grooves of his mind and society is sure to sink into the deepest labyrinth of his limited knowledge. This kind of knowledge is nothing short of a rebellion of the purest and best of creatures against the Creator. Knowledge based mainly on man's instincts, customs, avarice, egoism, pride and false teachings is not knowledge but sedition. The main task of the prophets was, therefore, to restore human nature to what it should be under the Will and all-embracing Love of the "Protecting Friend".

The concept of "Protecting Friend" first occurs in the *Quran* in the context of light and darkness.

> Allah is the Protecting Friend of those who believe. He bringeth them out of darkness into light. And for those who disbelieve, their patrons are false deities. They bring them out of light into darkness. Such are rightful owners of the Fire. They will abide therein.[6]

This verse follows three connecting verses. While in the first verse charity is enjoined upon believers (lest they should hoard), the second called the "Verse of the Throne" *(Ayat-ul-Kursi)* beautifully encapsulates the self-subsisting and eternal life, the activity and glory of Allah in the context of His absolute knowledge not bound by time or space. His eternal knowledge and our knowledge of Him and His creation are therefore two distinct categories of thought. It is in this sense that Allah is *Alim al-Ghaib*. The traditional interpretation of *ghaib* is Unseen. But we believe that *ghaib* includes both imperceptible and perceptible. This is why even in knowing we know nothing. The very fact that we have been fond of parading our disagreements on identical issues of an academic nature at lavish international conferences and seminars merely testifies to the limits both of our reason and knowledge. Human knowledge gets some "reflection of Reality" when it is in harmony with the Will and Plan of Allah. Since the knowledge that we seek to learn cannot be imposed from above, the verse following the "Verse of the Throne" exhorts:

> Let there be no compulsion in religion: Truth stands out clear from error: Whoever rejects anything worshipped beside Allah *(Tagut)* and believes in Allah, hath grasped the most trustworthy. Hand-hold *(Urwat ul-Wuthka)*, that never breaks. And Allah heareth and knoweth all things.[7]

It follows that the path we have chosen to follow is not hazardous but straight. So long as we tread this path and hold fast to it, not only is our protection amidst the snares and dangers of the world ensured, but what is more, our knowledge of ourselves will continue to grow by leaps and bounds. On the basis of his travels, experiences and knowledge, the author of the Persian classic, *Gulistan* remarks:

> I have not seen a seeker (of knowledge) losing direction,
> While objectively following the Truth.

The first creation of Allah is the light or knowledge. In fact, it was the knowledge of the Absolute that preceded the creation of Adam with matter and infusion of spirit into him. So long as Adam's activity was in accord with the Will of Allah, his home was heaven. But the moment Adam allowed himself to be guided by the reason of the Satan, Allah shifted his abode temporarily to the phenomenal world. The world we live in is therefore a step-by-step instruction manual. The key to understanding it is provided by both Adam's error of judgment and his subsequent repentance. Stepping into Adam's shoes is the only dignified way of living in the world. Realising this truth, Allama Iqbal remarks:

> The rise of clay-made Adam (after repentance) makes the star tremble
> Lest this fallen star becomes (as perfect as) full moon.[8]

The meaning of our presence in this world does not therefore depend upon our worldly possessions but is hidden in the light of our sense and soul to recognise the nothingness of our terrestrial splendour. From the standpoint of the *Quran*, our existence on this planet acquires meaning only in relation to our righteousness. The world would not have become a Utopia in the absence of economic disparities. Surely, economics has a marginal role to play in determining the formation of a personality. However, it cannot be denied that an acute sense of poverty and insecurity *vis-a-vis* affluence and security in human societies has always created certain mental states capable of moulding human beings in specified conditions. Contrary to the modern prophet of the economic revolution, the *Quran* does not construct a synthetic model of monolithic classless society. Given the human abnormalities of the social conditions in varied geographical and historical conditions as main propellents in the development of societies, human responses to the challenges of space and time have always varied. The spatio-temporal factors have therefore produced divisions, distinctions and inequities natural to this world as a prologeman to the next world. The social philosophy of eradicating this world of all its ills—poverty, hunger, illiteracy and inequity—is therefore not more than a Utopian dream. Thus the ideological obsession with creating a classless society is tantamount to prolongation of the agony of our living in an ephemeral world of infirmities and inequities. The break-up of the Communist world has amply demonstrated the futility of defining the world of man merely in material terms. Viewed in this context the recurrent Quranic concept of concern for the needs of the poor and ailing in the direction of creating a welfare society can be better understood than expounded. Compassion in the heart for human suffering is the guiding principle that the *Quran* stresses for building a bridge of understanding between the haves and have-nots. This is why every good act is described in the *Quran* not only as charity but also duty. The kindliest thought and act alone can convert darkness into light, ignorance into order, and above all ephemerality into eternity. The welfare society of the *Quran* rests on the principle of right and wrong rather than that of 'Might is right'. The failure of Communism needs to be understood in the latter sense. Isn't the dictatorship of the proletariat a totalitarian concept? Doesn't totalitarianism aim at suppressing initiative and individuality? Is there any scope for the development of personality in a totalitarian state?

The level of spiritual development of a personality therefore does not assuredly depend upon material possessions. This is the reason that poverty was broadly interpreted by the sages of most religions as a necessary stage in a thoughtful individual's spiritual development.[9] However, every individual is not a thoroughly developed individual in a spiritual sense. Even in this world we live in two different worlds—the world of an individual and that of individuals comprising societies or nations. The richer the spiritual development of individual personality, the profounder the differences between him and the society he lives in. The rate of his individual development is far greater than that of his society. Always conscious of the eternal fact that he has been created in the best of moulds, the activities of his spiritio-social consciousness are directed towards creating the meaningful bonds of affinity between himself and his environment. Adaptation rather than destruction guides the unbreakable rhythm of his inner time or consciousness. The richer the personality the greater the possibility for understanding his mission. The poorer the personality, the poorer prospects for establishing a rapport with him. In fact, no task is more difficult than to analyse the constitution of poorer personalities. Modern political and politio-religious leaders mostly fall within the category of complex mental personalities. The complexity of their personalities is such that they can be classified into several more categories in accordance with their egoistic, ethnocentric, mental, moral and avowedly universal religious characteristics. The structural relationship between the modern leadership and the masses is dependent not on hope but fear. Little wonder, then, that in a state of fear and psychosis the destruction of the human and ecological environment assumes a form condemnable in both religious and social terms. Still worse, the exploited in the process of ending social exploitation, commit naked and shameless acts of barbarous cruelty. While this stark reality is more pronounced among people or nations clamouring for justice, or a change of government, or their suppressed political aspirations or rights in contemporary situation, the history of the great revolutions of world history has a gruesome story to tell about the atrocities committed in the name of justice. In fact, every revolution has had bloodstained and blood-curdling significance. The revolutionaries have generally been bloodthirsty heroes in the historical drama.

The Glorious Revolution of 1688 is, of course, an exception to the rule. It was bloodless. True, the British statesmanship carried the revolution into learning, education and manners, but this very fact ultimately proved to be a major propellant in spreading the tentacles of British imperialism in Asia and Africa. The Industrial Revolution in England would not have produced results of far-reaching consequences had the general intellectual ferment of the eighteenth and nineteenth century not kept up the blood-circulation in the cold climate of England. How was the world to be conquered? How were its resources to be exploited for the industrial growth of a 'civilised' nation? Didn't the 'civilised' nation have the right to subjugate 'uncivilised' nations? Didn't the British have the right to direct and guide the 'uncivilised' in all spheres of life? Weren't the religions of the East—Buddhism, Hinduism and Islam—outmoded in contrast to the historical culmination of Christianity in Protestantism and its social ethics? Such questions, more or less, are crucial to our understanding of the intellectual barriers that imperialism created between man and man, religion and religion, nation and nation, and worse still, man and God. The violence of the outrages accompanying the Glorious and the Industrial Revolutions may be particularly gauged from the English literature on the "Orient" characterised by an innate sense of intellectual arrogance and hubris.

However disastrous the results of imperialism on Asia and Africa, there was a silver lining in the cloud of the colossus empire. English education led to a new spirit of enquiry in colonies. Although the response of subjugated people, in the form of a nationalist struggle, to imperialism has been eloquently and elaborately discussed in several historical works, much needs to be explored in the domain of the nature of conversions to Christianity during the colonial period. The most plausible view is the social nature of conversions. It was, by and large, the lower groups of the Hindu society and former Hindu converts to Islam, who were evangelised. But this change evoked a far spirited response to imperialism on the part of Hindus and Muslims than the British occupation of the subcontinent did. The socio-religious movements (Arya Samaj, Brahmo Samaj and 'Wahabi') among Hindus and Muslims therefore originated more from ideological than merely from religious foundations. What characterises the attempts of modern religious leaders (aptly called reformers) was not to restore the soul of the individual but to establish the ideological identity of their groups and movements. Their criticism of the irrational behaviour of the devotees of shrines and temples, though not without a sound reason was, in essence, a pathological obsession with what they perceived to be an imminent threat to Islam and Hinduism from the self-proclaimed rationality of Christian missionaries. Viewed in this context, imperialism cut at the very root of their identity, culture and personality consciousness in moulding the religious attitudes on the supposed purity of the rationality of belief rather than on a deeper spiritio-social cohesiveness fostered by the shrines through the centuries of Islamic acculturation.

That Muslims are entrenched in the colonial mesh and mess can hardly be denied. They may take pride in calling themselves servants of Allah but the fact remains that their relationship with the Creator is determined not so much by an inner urge to know the deeper truth as by their political or ideological attitudes. Thus, for the reconstruction of their personalities, Muslims need to re-orient their thinking and affiliation to the party of Allah (*Hizb Allah*) in the Quranic[10] rather than any contemporary political or ideological sense.

Before we reconstruct the model of personality as envisaged in the *Quran*, it is necessary to note that we shall refer to only such revelations as are clear (*muhkamat*) in contrast to allegorical (*mutashabihat*).[11] However, our attempt would not be to interpret these verses outside the integrated contextual structure of the *Quran*. The fundamental reason behind the *Quran's* criticism of the Jews and Christians is mainly that "they change words from their context..."[12] Again, it is important to remember that from the standpoint of the *Quran* Muslims alone are not believers. The believing Christian or a Jew may not be called a Muslim as commonly understood. But does this very disqualification ostracise devout Christians or Jews from the religion of Abraham (*Din-i Hanif*)? Muslims may differ on several points with the *ahl-i-kitab* for their flagrant violations of the *Shari'a* of the Torah and the *Bible* not to speak of their transgressions in terms of the *Quran*. But despite these differences, how can the noble actions of Christians and Jews for promoting peace and welfare on this planet escape the all-pervading notice of Allah? For this reason we take the verse enjoining upon Muslims and non-Muslims to vie with each other in righteousness[13] as the very basis for remaking the human personality in this strife-torn world.

Let us understand the meaning of righteousness through the words of Allah: "It is not righteousness that ye turn your faces towards East or West; but it is righteousness to believe in Allah and the Last Day, and the Angels, and the Book, and the Messengers; to spend of your substance, out of love for Him, for your kin, for orphans, for the needy, for the wayfarer, for those who ask, and for the ransom of slaves, to be steadfast in prayer, and give *zakat*, to fulfil the contracts which ye have made; and to be firm and patient, in pain (or suffering) and adversity, and throughout all periods of panic. Such are the people of truth, the God-fearing."[14]

The significance of prayer *(salat)* in the direction of K'aba has been repeatedly emphasized in the *Quran* not merely in terms of one of the fundamentals of the Abrahamic religion but also in the context of its perfection in the ascension of the personality of Muhammad *(mi'raj)*. True, in the context of the *Quran* devout Muslims the world over turn towards Ka'ba in vindication of their belief in the Oneness of Allah *(Tawhid)* and the unity of Muslim believers *(umma)*, but the question that one may ask strictly within the parameters of the Quranic consciousness is whether Muslims exhibit similar or uniform degree of spiritual wakefulness during the course of prayer. Since this question has no affirmative answer, Muslim prayer has a deeper significance than that of being a mere ritual act.

A ritual act is either a ceremonial one or a religiously prescribed mode of behaviour. Prayer is a ritual, but when we reflect on the *Quran's* repeated emphasis on its daily performance five times a day at regular intervals, the whole gamut of our spiritual consciousness experiences a sense of duty towards the Creator and the created. The daily prayer dutifully performed transforms the human personality from its specific individuality into a universal personality. Such a personality has distinctive, especially socially attractive, qualities uniting not only its own person but, also, those exposed to its radiant influences and to the Creator. The man of God therefore does not have a weak personality. His personality is not only strong but also likeable. True believers need him not for leading a ceremonial act but for nourishing and fostering the development of their personalities. It is in this context that the religious leader *(imam)* assumes supreme significance in Islam.

As the deputies of his mission, Muhammad expected the *ulama* to cast their personalities in his mould. Islam has no place for priesthood, nor does it sanctify the personality of an *imam* by virtue of his office or heredity. Yet it is common knowledge that the *ulama* have almost become counterparts of the Christian or Jewish priests *vis-a-vis* their commitment to theological institutions and their versions of Islam. Their activities focus on dissemination of purely theological knowledge among Muslims besides performance of religious duties as *imams* and *khatibs* of the mosques. Generally, a majority of the *ulama* have a very little knowledge of *Tawhidic Weltanschuung* considering their roots in the traditional seminaries which have no place for the so-called secular subjects like natural and social sciences in their curricula. Consequently, the *ulamas'* vision of Islam is fossilised. Having followed the compartmentalisation of knowledge into sacred and profane in the Western fashion, the *ulama* have been largely responsible for much of the social malaise and atrophy characterising the Muslim societies.

One of the significant features of the priesthood is the division of the human personality into sacred and secular. A priest in Christianity and Judaism, or, for that matter, in Hinduism and Buddhism, is markedly distinguishable not only by his functions but even dress. His functions are well defined according to the mundane concept of the division of labour. A certain degree of sanctity, or social respectability that centres round a priest is due more to the religious duties performed by him which otherwise would not be performed in his absence. The existence of a hierarchy in the organisation of the management of the churches is a point worthy of consideration in respect of the classification of men devoted to God. In England, the High Church, a section of the Church, itself emphasises ritual and the authority of bishops and priests.

The *Quran*, as I understand it, invests every individual with the authority of spiritual leadership[15] provided he not only responds to Allah's exhortations but consecrates his thought and actions to their explanation. The relevance of the *Quran* for rebuilding human personality in every age and environment can be recognised only when an individual represents the universality of the man of the *Quran* in his person. Such an individual is an example in human form of several qualities or

characteristics that emanate from the source itself. A brief
explanation is necessary. Allah has several names *(asma)*, or more
appropriately characteristics, the most commonly invoked being
the Most Beneficent and the Most Merciful. An individual may be
named the servant of the Most Beneficent *(Abd al-Rahman)* or the
servant of the the Most Merciful *(Abd al-Rahim)*. Such names are
common but how many of these souls realise the significance of
their inner relationship with their Nourisher *(Rabb)*? The question
applies to every individual, no matter whether he bears such a
name or not. The moment he moves in the direction of
recognising his covenant with Allah he begins to turn into a
source of energy. Weren't there individuals in the history of Islam
who personified such eternal sources of energy as mercifulness,
beneficence, kindness, and several other divine characteristics?
What made them proteges of God? What accorded a special
charm to their personalities? Weren't (or aren't) they different
from the best known personalities in the world of history,
politics, sports and films? Before we revert to the exposition of
these issues let us have a nodding but reflective acquaintance
with the men of science.

It is necessary to understand men of science as creative
personalities in more than one important sense. They are
dedicated individuals who continue to serve humankind in
several respects. The majority of them may not be believers but
through their researches they have fortified our belief in the
infiniteness of the cosmos, not to speak of the Creator's
unfathomable Infinity. If I were asked about my preferences in
respect of company, I would prefer to spend my leisure in the
company of the social and natural scientists rather than the ones
who have ready-made answers concerning religion *vis-a-vis* the
problems of societies on the move. The natural and social
scientists have enquiring minds whereas the spirit of enquiry is
decried in theology. Little wonder, then, that *taqlidi ulama* appear
to me veritable wonders of theology rather than religion. I have
argued before that theology was the necessary corollary of Islam
in its historical manifestation a century or so after the demise of
the Prophet. In fact, Islam owes its historical resilience to various
onslaughts to four schools of theological thought that emerged
during a period of great crisis. But then the morbid growth of
Muslim societies is explicable in terms of the latter-day *ulamas'*

infatuation with theology rather than the intrinsic enquiring spirit of the *Quran*.

While I am deeply conscious of the futility of opening the doors of *ijtihad* in respect of the clear injunctions of the *Quran* regarding the fundamentals of Islam, none the less, I hold a contrary view on the current debate concerning this issue of contemporary relevance. I think that *ijtihad* has not been a matter of historical prerogative merely exercised by the four venerable teachers of Islamic history. The less known and less understood fact is that *ijtihad* has been the guiding factor in the development or underdevelopment of Muslim societies in several respects. When the four great *imams* exercised the right to *ijtihad* on innumerable issues concerning religion *vis-a-vis* society they ensured the social stability and resilience of Islam against various challenges. Consequently, Islam flourished no matter what one's affiliation to one school or the other. But when in the course of the development of Muslim societies theology became an obsession rather than a creative process in the depths of one's soul and mind, it became a byword for stagnation rather than excellence. It was on this score that the Sufis differed from *ulama* in more than one respect. As a matter of fact, the four *imams* had the courage of conviction, not unlike most Sufis, not to associate themselves with the government. And some of them suffered for their *de facto* defiance of the un-Islamic governments. The four great theologians of Islam, like Sufis, thus belong to the category of *Ulama-i-haqq* as against *Ulama-i dunniya* or *Ulama-i su*.

Traditionally, the *Ulama-i su* or *Ulama-i dunniya* have been condemned for their association with the State power for accepting government jobs. But we need to probe into the deeper reasons for their denunciation by no less men of integrity and character than the Sufis. Our study reveals that they became the object of ridicule for accepting land grants from the state for living a life of ease and comfort, for misinterpreting the *Shari'a*, for giving religious legitimacy to the despotic government, for ignoring their social responsibilities, for being engines of oppression in suppressing the voice of dissent against misrule and social exploitation, for giving birth to hair-splitting controversies with the main purpose of serving their vested interests rather than those of *din*, for fostering the negative forces such as hatred, discord and revenge as sources of energy, and above all, for their mechanical view of religion. Although innumerable historical works and Sufis can be quoted to substantiate my argument about the *ulama-i su,* it will suffice here to quote the best of Kashmiri Sufi master's views on their negative role:

> Indeed, the only theologian (worth the name) was Maulana Rumi
>
> Otherwise, seek the refuge of Allah on seeing a theologian.[17]

That many Sufis like Shaikh Nuruddin Rishi Kashmiri regarded the *Ullama-i su* as personifications of the devil can be hardly denied. Such *ulama* have always existed in Muslim societies. Their chief avocation, as the avowed guardians of the Prophet's mission, has been not to nourish, humanise, refine and deepen personalities but to limit their inborn capacities for spiritual growth by administering them a dose of fear psychosis. But a well-articulated challenge from outside forces to the Muslim societies—be it technological, economic, social, political and anti-religious—is not fear. Such a challenge or challenges need to be debated in a true academic spirit for generating a renewed sense of spiritual and social awareness among Muslims. Unfortunately, however, Muslims have been least educated in that respect. The *ulamas'* concern for maintaining the identity of Muslims in the face of various odds is laudable. But haven't they used Muslim identity-consciousness for the multiple mundane interests of their groups and institutions rather than the higher universal aims of *din*? Neither the *Quran* nor the *Sunna* call for a massive operation like rousing mobs into anger in the name of Islam. The mentality of the mob is the anti-thesis of the *Quran* and the *Sunna.* The ultimate aim of *din* is to enable every individual to prove his identity as a sublime force of *Tawhidic* unity, identity, and stability. This concept of personality is neither alien to Islam nor divorced from its manifestations during the historical evolution of Muslim societies. As the poet-philosopher of the subcontinent remarks:

> With him (the Muslim) the spiritual basis of life is a matter of conviction for which even the least enlightened man among us can easily lay down his life; and in view of the basic idea of Islam that there can be no further revelation binding on man, we ought to be spiritually one of the most emancipated

peoples on earth. Early Muslims, emerging out of the spiritual slavery of pre-Islamic Asia, were not in a position to realise the true significance of this basic idea. Let the Muslim of today appreciate his position, reconstruct his social life in the light of ultimate principle, and evolve, out of the hitherto partially revealed purpose of Islam, that spiritual democracy which is the ultimate aim of Islam."[18]

Notes and References

1. "We sent thee not, but as a Mercy for all creatures." *Quran*, 21/107.
2. Ibid., 85/14.
3. Of course, the Prophet Muhammad and his four pious companions also headed governments; but such governments, to borrow the phraseology of Allama Mohammad Iqbal, were "spiritual democracies" rather than governments as understood in the Western political or ideologically-oriented Islamic sense. In the latter context, Maulana Maududi describes the Islamic system as a "theo-democracy" distinguishable from a theocracy or clerical state, in which the popular will is made subservient to and "limited by God's law". While Maududi found no difficulty in characterising an Islamic government or theo-democracy as "Islamic totalitarianism", Iqbal, as Espositio rightly points out, "sought to 'rediscover' the Islamic principles and values that provide the basis for Islamic versions of Western concepts and institutions such as democracy and parliamentary government." *The Islamic Threat*, p. 60. It must be borne in mind that for Iqbal "a spiritual interpretation of the universe, spiritual emancipation of the individual, and basic principles of a universal import directing the evolution of human society on a spiritual basis" are essential for the success of "spiritual democracy", and "which is the ultimate aim of Islam'. *The Reconstruction of Religious Thought in Islam*, pp. 179-80. It is significant that Iqbal did not stand for totalitarianism of any kind: "...we (Muslims) ought to be spiritually one of the most emancipated peoples on earth", in striking contrast to "intolerant democracies" of Europe. Ibid., Isn't Iqbal's view more in consonance with the spirit of the *Quran* and *Sunna* than that of Maulana Maududi?
4. Maulana Azad and Maulana Maududi.
5. *Quran*, 95/4-7.
6. Ibid., 2/257.
7. Ibid., 2/256.
8. *Kuliyat-i-Iqbal*, Urdu, p. 302.

9. For a detailed discussion on this theme, see Ishaq Khan, *Kashmir's Transition to Islam.*

10. For the author's comment on Kenneth Cragg's understanding of *Hizb Allah,* see *Journal of the Institute of Muslim Minority Affairs,* Vol. XII, No: 1st January 1991, London, p. 174.

11. *Quran,* 3/7.

12. Ibid., 6/13.

13. Ibid.

14. Ibid., 2/177.

15. The Quranic prayer is worthy of quotation here: "...Our Lord! Grant unto us wives and offspring who will be the comfort of our eyes, and give us (the grace) to lead the righteous." This prayer follows verses 63-73 of the Chapter XXV entitled the Criterion *(Furqan):* "The verses have been aptly described as a 'fine code of individual and social ethics', a ladder of spiritual development, open to all". See *The Holy Quran,* tr. Allama Yusuf Ali, n. 3135.

16. Fazlur Rahman rightly observes that "every person and every people have continuously to search their own consciences, and, because of this engraving upon their hearts, which represents the primordial Covenant, none may take refuge in the excuse that they had been preconditioned by their 'hereditary memory', by the set ways of 'our forefathers'. The primary task of the prophets is to awaken man's conscience so that he can decipher the primordial writing on his heart more clearly and with great conviction." *Themes of the Quran,* Oxford, p. 25. Although Allah elicited "primordial covenant" from all men *(Quran,* 7/172), He took a specially "solemn Covenant" from the Prophets—Noah, Abraham, Moses, Jesus, and Muhammad. See Ibid., 33/7.

17. *Kuliyat-i-Shaikh al-Alam,* published by Jammu and Kashmir Academy of Art, Culture and Languages, Srinagar, 1985, pp. 128-29. See also *Kashmir's Transition to Islam,* p. 112

18. Iqbal, op. cit., pp. 179-80.

10

THE FLOWERING OF PERSONALITY

"What concern hath Allah for your punishment if ye are thankful (for His mercies) and believe (in Him)? Allah was ever Responsive, Aware."[1] The more an individual reflects on this verse, the more he is able to realise in the depths of his growing spiritual consciousness that he is an inseparable part of the Universal Consciousness. An expression of thanks for small courtesies is part of our normal behaviour. Millions of men and women thank each other in their daily conversation, correspondence and other forms of social behaviour. Life would be dull and dreary if we stop making friendly gestures in our human relations. As a matter of fact, the development of both personalities and societies is in no small measure affected by our individual friendly actions and responses. It is not therefore difficult to understand why Allah wants our thinking and actions to be in harmony with the ethical principles of the Quran. Any deviation from the universal ethics of the Quran is bound to create disharmony in our human relations; and this is why the Quran repeatedly brings home to us the significance of being conscious of our duty to Him and His creatures.

Seest thou one who denies the Judgement (to come)? Then such is the one who repulses the orphan, and encourages not the feeding of the indigent. So woe the worshippers who are neglectful of their prayers, those who (want but) to be seen, but refuse (to supply) (even) neighbourly needs.[2]

Thanksgiving has been highly valued in the Quran so much so that Allah remembers the one who always remembers Him.[3] The act of expressing thanks to Him through prayers, charity and several good acts is ordained for bringing an individual believer closer to an understanding of the purpose of creation. The primary objective behind the constant expression of thanks is in acknowledgement of the favours that Allah has bestowed on all human beings save those who are unable to think owing to some congenital disease or defect. Being a poor or destitute is not a disqualification in spiritual terms. Likewise, any physical defect does not disqualify an individual from remembering His Creator so long as he has consciousness, i.e., until the last breath. In modern times, the handicapped have been able to overcome most of their limitations, thanks to the advancement of learning. They have been able to earn a respectable living through individual efforts. What is more, some of them have even won worldwide recognition for their individual achievements. Here I may recall the names of Helen Keller (1880-1968) and Stephen W. Hawking. While the former distinguished herself as lecturer, author and educator despite her blindness and deafness from infancy, about the latter the *Time* magazine writes: "Even as he sits helpless in his wheelchair, his mind seems to soar ever more brilliantly across the vastness of space and time to unlock the secrets of the universe."

It is not therefore handicapped individuals who are mentally deficient, but paradoxically, individuals with seemingly sound physique and mind. They are so mainly because of their ungratefulness. Their inability to express gratitude is a sign of their feeble-mindedness to think. Thankfulness indeed indicates a disposition to express gratitude by giving thanks, as to the Beneficent and Merciful. There is often a sense of being delivered, liberated or salvaged as well as of thankfulness when a true believer remembers God. In fact, his gratefulness is the exemplification of his *Tawhidic* consciousness to realise that Allah guides whom He wills.[4]

Allah guideth not wrong doing folk.[5]
Allah guideth not the disbelieving folk.[6]
Had he willed He could indeed have guided all of you.[7]

It should not be construed from the above that the good or bad conduct of an individual hinges upon Allah's will. Only individuals with a superficial reading of the *Quran* can arrive at such a dangerous conclusion. The good and bad, indeed, in the context of the *Quran*, seem to me indispensable categories of the integrated Mind of the *Quran*. The Mind of the *Quran* intrinsically seeks to establish a meaningful relationship with the complex and variegated structures of the human mind. If the response of the human mind to the injunctions of the *Quran* is in harmony with its spiritio-social ethics, wisdom and grace will envelope it in unfathomable and immeasurable terms. It is in this sense that the prayers of the prophets for granting wisdom and grace from His presence *(ladunna)* need to be understood. And when a believer recites such prayers in all sincerity, humility and hope, Allah's wisdom and mercy surely unfolds itself, through gradual stages, in the flowering of such a personality. Being divinely guided, this type of personality is the most powerful source of energy for seekers after the Truth. It is the source of stability, harmony and peace in the world as against the average or ordinary mind not in congruity with the Universal Mind.

It follows that the good exists in harmony with its eternal Source whereas the evil is latent in the negative disposition of our minds to defy all that is universally good. It is in this respect that the *Quran* is quite explicit on the polarisation of our mental dispositions. "The evil and the good are not alike even though the plenty of the evil attract thee. So be mindful of your duty to Allah, men of understanding, that ye may succeed."[8]

From the standpoint of the *Quran,* men of understanding are not merely those who believe in Him but also those who constantly exercise their minds towards an understanding of their existence *vis-a-vis* the cosmos and its Creator. Two basic principles guide the thinking of those whom the *Quran* calls *ulul-al-bab*. First, such men are always conscious of their limitations in terms of both their knowledge of Him and His universe. "Have ye any knowledge of that you can adduce for us? Lo! ye follow naught but an opinion. Lo! ye do but guess."[9]

It needs little stressing that over the last several decades both social and physical scientists' researches and findings have shown the futility of discovering absolute laws governing the universe in either historical or scientific terms. As Stephen W. Hawking observes: "With the advent of quantum mechanics, we have come to recognise that events cannot be predicted with complete accuracy but that there is always a degree of uncertainty. If one likes, one could ascribe this randomness to the intervention: there is no evidence that it is directed towards any purpose. Indeed, if it were, it would by definition not be random. In modern times, we have effectively removed the possibility (of there being no theory of the universe; events cannot be predicted beyond a certain extent but occur in a random and arbitrary manner) by redefining the goal of science: our aim is to formulate a set of laws that enables us to predict events only up to the limit set by the uncertainty principle."[10]

Thus the insatiable thirst of the physical scientists to understand the origin of the universe is unlikely to be quenched in that the "uncertainty principle" is designed to crystallise and organise thinking in a manner that makes it subject to a continuous process of revision in the light of ceaseless thinking. Although a scientist does not fall within the category of a personality that emerges in the *Quran,* yet it would not be incorrect to say that the scientific or the so-called secular knowledge itself is the product of the creative evolution of the partial intellect of man. This explains the fact that while the pursuit of scientific research is no longer considered to be antithetical to religion, at the same time, the post-modernist[11] revulsion against the dominant ideological inheritances of the nineteenth century confirms our doubts about the absurdity of a mere human rationality claiming universality.

The second premise on which the Quranic model of personality conditions its mind is trust *(tawwakul).* Any human effort towards the fruition of a goal cannot bear fruit without faith. There are various forms of faith, viz., faith in Allah's bounty, in one's own individual capability, in the social solidarity of a particular nation or group bound together by common ties of ideology, in one's military and technological strength and supremacy and so on. Of these, faith in Allah's encompassing Grace alone constitutes the cornerstone of a believer's activity. Hence the verse: "And when thou art resolved, then put thy trust in Allah. Lo! Allah loveth those who put their trust (in Him)."[12]

Consciousness of our finiteness in relation to Allah's Infinity and His cosmos and a resolve to anchor our thinking in His encompassing Mind therefore provide us the keys to arriving at a deeper understanding of our purposeful existence. But our awareness of ourselves as longing models of the Quranic personality will increase by leaps and bounds only on realising that every good action of ours is the living essence not only of our spiritual nature but also the very foundation of our individual integrity throughout the minute processes of our interaction with our societies. The perpetual happiness of our inner life is the conviction that we are loved by Allah not merely for the impassioned love of our souls for Him but more for our inspired social actions. The greatest merit of the *Quran* is its exposition of love in objective rather than abstract terms. Love is the greatest of graces that Allah can vouchsafe to us, for He Himself is the Loving *(Wudud)*.[13] And our bond of love with Him will be nourished if we practise the simple but profound universal philosophy of love in our everyday life. In fact, our first step towards the realisation of the loftiest and most glorious ideal of human society in the context of model and ideal should be the beginning of a struggle within ourselves rather than against our so-called enemies. Let us, therefore, reflect on various verses, against the context of Allah's love for true believers, for an objective interpretation of a concept that captures the quintessence of the Quranic *Weltanschuung*.

> Fight in the cause of Allah against those who fight you, but do not transgress limits; for Allah loveth not transgressors.[14]
>
> Truly Allah loveth those who turn unto Him, and loveth those who have a care for cleanness.[15]
>
> And Allah guideth not wrong-doing folk.[16]
>
> Allah loveth not the disbelieving folk.[17]
>
> Allah loveth not the impious and guilty.[18]
>
> Allah is the Protecting Friend of the believers.[19]
>
> Allah loveth those who ward off (evil).[20]
>
> Allah loveth the good.[21]
>
> Allah loveth the steadfast.[22]
>
> Allah loveth those who put their trust (in Him).[23]
>
> Allah loveth the equitable.[24]
>
> Allah loveth not corrupters.[25]
>
> Allah loveth not the treacherous.[26]
>
> Allah loveth not prodigals.[27]
>
> Lo! my Protecting Friend is Allah who revealeth the Scripture. He befriendeth the righteous.[28]
>
> ...Allah is your Befriender—a transcendent Patron, a transcedent Helper.[29]

Lo! Allah loveth those who keep their duty (unto Him).[30]

Allah loveth the purifiers.[31]

And expend in the way of Allah; and cast not yourselves by your hands into destruction, but be good-doers; Allah loveth the good-doers.[32]

Allah loves the just dealers.[33]

Lo! Allah loves not any braggart boaster.[34]

Allah loves the equitable.[35]

Lo! Allah loves those who battle for His cause in ranks, as if they were a solid structure.[36]

The *Quran* is thus like a balance,[37] a "criterion" or "clearly demarcating line" *(furqan)*[38] enjoining believers to weigh all issues concerning social roles, all questions of right and wrong in conduct. They are constantly reminded of endeavouring in that direction since the judgment is inevitable. Being assigned a central position in the cosmos, man is bound to be accountable. "When earth is shaken with a mighty shaking and earth brings forth her burdens, and Man says, 'What ails her?' upon that day she shall tell her tidings for that her Lord has inspired her. Upon that day man shall issue in scatterings to see their (works), and whoso has done an atom's weight of good shall see it, and who so has done an atom's weight of evil shall see it."[39]

Being the Living Testament of Man's natural religion, the *Quran* is fundamentally an act of the divine Will as against mere act of thought and response that constitutes human history. When Allah willed, He created man. When He willed He chose his station in the heaven. When He willed He turned him out of the heaven to descend on this planet. When He willed, He created various nations out of the progeny of Adam. When He willed He sent various prophets for the guidance of mankind. When He willed He caused the destruction of various nations. When He willed He crowned the last of the prophets with the *Quran*. When he willed He caused the ascension *(mi'raj)* of Muhammad. The descent of Adam and the ascent of Muhammad are not therefore independent variables but, in essence, constitute the intrinsic truth connecting the Quranic model of personality with the glory and sublimity of a process we call divinito-human creativity. It is not the aim of the *Quran* to bring ideals into their concrete existence. But, surely, it is the purpose of Allah that human beings must perform such acts as may bring them closer to an understanding or approximation of a long-term ideal. It is in this sense that the Quranic model of personality consciously ascends into Allah's Presence at every moment of his mundane existence particularly during the prayers and, not the least, while rendering good to humanity.

Man is not the result of a sudden birth. For that reason even the birth of physically or mentally handicapped persons cannot be attributed to accidental factors. As a matter of fact, their very existence itself forms part of the purpose of creation in enabling the negligent to bestir themselves to the good of humankind. Likewise, millions of people who are at the subsistence level or far below the poverty line merely represent a state of life in the divine drama to make the rich conscious of their spiritual and social obligations. Human life is, in the totality of all its variegated aspects, full of complexities as well as moral responsibilities. The meaning and purpose of mundane existence is, therefore, embedded in an incessant struggle for coordination and perfection of its spiritual and material aspects.

Perfection may be an elusive concept in terms of a social system or social order, but certainly not so in the context of an individual's spiritual existence. The *Quran* and the *Sunna* of Muhammad bear elaborate testimony to the fact of individual perfection in our earthly existence in spiritual rather than material terms. Of course, it is not the purpose of the *Quran* to produce the replica of the Meccan and the Medini life of the Prophet in the life cycles of his followers living in societies whose history is tangibly different in a specific time and place. However, it must be borne in mind that the *Quran* and the *Sunna* have provided the key to everything which happened in Muslim societies during their periods of historical evolution. The relative strength or weakness of Muslim personalities has therefore also lain hidden in the idea as to how far the universality of Islam was carried forward or pushed to the background by their adherence to the 'model' and 'ideal' in individual lives or *vice versa*.

It follows that Islam is essentially a matter of individual ethical responsibility seeking entrance for men into the eternal reality beyond the ephemeral complexities, mysteries and appearances of the world. It is a deepening process of life within the encompassing bounds of the *Quran* and the *Sunna* aimed at raising man out of the limits of physical time to ascend into the sphere of Infinity.

However, historical knowledge, divorced from the spiritual, is finite. For the spirit of *din* revives, and history becomes meaningful only when societies respond to religion, no matter whether positively, negatively or tepidly. The Western European nations lay in their sepulchres, until awakened by the renewed maturity of the Abrahamic religion. The West's response to Islam was not spiritual but merely mental or temporal in contrast to Asian and African societies. Western historical thought, though based on the foundations of a revolt of the Western mind against Catholicism, none the less, in the course of its development, arrayed itself against Islam. Western Orientalist studies on Islam were inspired mainly by such dominant concepts of Western thought as syncretism, culture and civilisation rather than the creative spirit of the *Shari'a* that regulated or influenced the development of Muslim societies. Histories were produced to serve the conceptual, ideological and imperialist concerns as well as ingrained hubristic habits of mind. Islam thus became a thought in the thought processes of Western rationalists, but described and analysed only in misapplied, misconceived and abstract words.

The most dangerous result of the rationalisation of Islam in the Western categories of thought was the popularisation of the notion of the progressive mind of the West in strikingly dramatised contrast to the misunderstood mental journey of Muslims backward through time. Expressed differently: what rational development of personality meant to the man in the West did not carry the same meaning with the man in the so-called Muslim world.

The concept of man in the *Quran* is that of a potential vicegerent of God on this planet, and it is accordingly meaningless to set rational limits to what he is capable of being even in the so-called irrational terms. The rational and irrational are not, therefore, objective tools of understanding for the concept of a personality that emerges in the *Quran*. Although human beings are gifted with the reasoning mind, there are innumerable layers of structures within the structure of the mind.

These structures have a close interaction with one's belief, instincts, emotions, sentiments, moorings, upbringing, heredity, environment and so on. This is also the reason that our perceptions of ourselves widely differ. Had it been possible for us to arrive at a syncretic or mutual understanding of ourselves in rational terms, our world would have since turned into an Utopia. But the fact is that the polarisation of our perceptions in varied contexts of our rationalities alone accounts for our existence in innumerable ephemeral worlds of our mentalities. In our analysis, then, man ceases to be rational or irrational in the context of the *Quran*. On the other hand, he emerges in the broadening horizon of our spiritio-social consciousness as an entity intrinsically cast in a natural mould. It is not therefore difficult to understand why the *Quran* describes Islam as *din-al-fitra*[40] rather than a religion based on pure reason. Of course the *Quran* lays great stress on the intellect of man, but not to the extent of rationalising it in order to produce a perfect human model of rationality. Notwithstanding the Prophet Muhammad's personality as a paragon of perfect human excellence, the act of repentance *(tauba)* forms the distinguishing trait of his *Sunna*. Therefore, the cardinal rationale behind the Quranic emphasis on repentance *(tauba)* is the one that relates to unsuperable limitations of partial human rationality amputated from its Source.

The limits *(hudud)*[41], in the context of the *Quran*, appear to me a significant and original concept of abiding value. It is indeed incomprehensible to understand the flowering of human personality *vis-a-vis* the *Quran* without the concept of limits to human reason. The *Quran* prescribes certain limits for man's development in intellectual and social terms. Whether he adheres to the norms of the *Quran* or not, his personality in either case is moulded in a natural form. Being part and parcel of the divine or natural process, man enjoys full freedom to respond to the Will of Allah in consonance with His *Shari'a* or respond to His Will within the narrow confines of his rationality. Human existence, therefore, becomes purposeful and intelligible only within the limits of the *Shari'a* of the *Quran*. And, but for this consciousness man would have been an automaton. So robotic has been the movement of human reason that morality has become a taboo in the West in relation to the rational pontificating about free sex, sodomy and the trade in pornography.

From the standpoint of the *Shari'a* as a moral code[42], man's reason is directly or indirectly, or, in other words, intentionally or unintentionally, involved in every human action. And it is this inbuilt faculty of the human mind that makes the Day of Judgment comprehensible to us within the limits of our rationality. Our actions, both in terms of variegated intentional structures of our mentalities and socialities will be judged in a widely encompassing and integrated concept of Divine Justice. In this sense our understanding of human rationality is directly opposed to its ordinary definition, but remains intrinsically a matter of intentionality. Hence the prophetic dictum:

Verily the deeds are to be judged by intentions.[43]

Human intentions need to be qualified. Unless they are designated as good or bad, individual or collective, particular or universal, idealistic or materialistic, personal or impersonal, egoistic or altruistic it would be impossible to promote a better understanding of the human personality *vis-a-vis* the *Quran*. It is in this sense that we may reflect deeply on a very significant verse: "Say each one doth according to his rule of conduct, and thy Lord is best aware of him whose way is right."[44]

Here the concept of Islam or surrender to Allah emerges as a matter of human attitudes within the widening limits of His *Shari'a*. *Seen from this perspective the concept of Shari'a or limits itself appears as a progressive concept in respect of how a believer relates it to his everyday intentionalities and actions.* Thus every interpretation of *Shari'a*, in the context of the *Quran*, needs to be understood as a form of natural response of man within the limits of his natural understanding. And the *Quran* places a high value on such an understanding or consciousness in these words: "He giveth wisdom unto whom He will, and he unto whom wisdom is given, he truly hath received abundant good. But none remember except men of understanding."[45]

In the Quranic sense, therefore, it is the natural law of religion, or, in other words, ethicality rather than rationality that is binding on human conduct in any given social system.

Nature is far deeper a relevant concept than that of rationalism. The latter is an outgrowth of history whereas the former remains an inseparable part of the Divine Will. It is not the aim of the *Quran* to rationalise the behaviour of humans in the

Western sense; rather its primary object is to produce a consciousness within the blended nexus of the soul and mind for humanisation or dehumanisation of the man in natural terms. The Quranic emphasis on intellect thus forms an integral part of the mundane ephemerality rather than the sole criterion for judging the divine creativity and inevitability in rationalistic terms. The rationality embodying the Mind of the *Quran* is not rationality as commonly understood but radiancy. Not only the divine Reason, but, also, the divine Love encompasses the divine Grace. In this sense, repentance *(tauba)* for our dehumanised behaviour marks the beginning of a consciousness of a higher degree for realising our basic nature as a first step towards the exaltation of our personalities in the estimation of Allah. The transmutation of individual personalities from one state of consciousness to another is, therefore, neither dramatic nor rationalistic but a rejuvenating, rekindling and radiating process in their continuing lifecycles *vis-a-vis* societies. There are of course grades or ranks for each individual with Allah[46] for his response to His Will in the form of his own rule of conduct, or in other words, the natural and habitual inclination of his mind. It is not, therefore, justifiable, in the context of the *Quran* and the *Sunna,* to condemn believers in the Oneness of Allah, no matter whatever their religion, to hell. The *Quran* reserves the act of finally judging the actions of individuals to none other than Allah. Viewed against this background, love of the Creator and the created permeating the consciousness of prophets and sufis, makes itself comprehensible in the wider and deepest framework of the *Tawhidic Weltanschuung.* Even the natural scientists' labour of love for alleviating the sufferings of humanity cannot be lost sight of in the deepest and infinite profundities of Allah's awareness of actions of all creatures inhabiting His universe.

The flowering of the concept of personality in the *Quran* is thus a concrete reality within the universal framework of the *Tawhidic* consciousness rather than within the confines of a rationality or its synonym, particularity. The limitations of human consciousness become manifest when man begins hostilities, even though paradoxically, in the name of religious particularities or, for that matter, even the secular, liberal or the orchestrated progressive ideologies. Nothing undermines the strength of a personality more seriously than the conflicts central

to the dialectic of fear, threat or aggrandisement of every kind
nourished and fostered by a particular rationality. Although fear
of God is essential for the cultivation of hope and indomitable
spirit, the fear of nations or groups against one another is at the
root of conflicts of cankerous ideological nature. Unless man
learns to banish this kind of feeble fear from his mind, he would
not be able to discover his universality within his own soul.

The most excellent chapter of human history is the one
related to the Prophet Muhammad. Didn't he start his religious
career on the eternal foundations of an insatiable desire to know
the Truth rather than on imaginary and baseless fears of one kind
of human rationality against another? The desire to comprehend
the Truth always requires an incessant and integrated effort of
the human mind and soul in unison against the snares of self and
reason. Such a form of human endeavour is termed *jihad-i akbar* in
the *Quran*. Since it is incumbent upon Allah to respond to such
souls and minds, hence the divine assurance of help, protection
and sustenance for them in these words:

> Lo! verily the friends of Allah are (those) on whom fear
> (cometh) not, nor do they grieve:
> Those who believe and keep their duty (to Allah), Theirs are
> good tidings in the life of the world and in the Hereafter—
> There is no changing the words of Allah—that is the Supreme
> Triumph.[47]

Notes and References

1. *Quran*, 5/147.
2. Ibid., 107/1-7.
3. Ibid., 2/52.
4. Ibid., 6/88.
5. Ibid., 2/258.
6. Ibid., 2/264.
7. Ibid., 6/149.
8. Ibid., 7/100.
9. Ibid., 8/149.
10. Stephen W. Hawkings, *A Brief History of Time*, Bantam Books, New York, 1989, pp. 176-77.
11. Although post-modernism seems to me to represent a deepening crisis of human rationality within its pigeon-holes, its relevance in respect of the Quran's emphasis on the need to understand the Unity of Allah and the diversity of beliefs, ideas and ways cannot be

ignored. Akbar S. Ahmed rightly emphasises the germaneness of postmodernism to Islam. See Ahmad, *Postmodernism and Islam: Predicament and Promise*, Penguin Books India, 1993.

12. *Quran*, 4/159; 64/13 etc.
13. Ibid., 85/14.
14. Ibid., 2/190.
15. Ibid., 2/222.
16. Ibid., 2/258.
17. Ibid., 2/264.
18. Ibid., 2/276; 3/31-32.
19. Ibid., 3/68.
20. Ibid., 3/76.
21. Ibid., 3/134; 3/148; 7/193.
22. Ibid., 4/146; 8/46; 8/66.
23. Ibid., 4/159.
24. Ibid., 6/12.
25. Ibid., 6/64.
26. Ibid., 7/87; 8/55.
27. Ibid., 6/142; 7/31
28. Ibid., 9/196.
29. Ibid., 8/40.
30. Ibid., 9/4; 9/17; 9/36.
31. Ibid., 9/108; 9/123.
32. Ibid., 2/195.
33. Ibid., 60/8.
34. Ibid., 31/18
35. Ibid., 49/9
36. Ibid., 61/4
37. Ibid., 42/17; 57/25.
38. The *Quran* grants a criterion to a man for distinguishing right from wrong in the worldly environment. The spiritual, human and ecological concern of a true believer is deep-rooted in the ethos of the culture of the *Quran*.
39. *Quran*, 99/1-8.
40. "So set they purpose (O Muhammad) for religion as a man by nature upright—the nature (framed) of Allah, in which He hath created man. There is no altering (the laws of) all Allah's creation. That is the right religion, but most men know not." Ibid., 30/30.
41. Ibid., 2/187; 229/4/13
42. See Ishaq Khan, *Kashmir's Transition to Islam*.
43. *Tajrid al-Bukhari*, part I, p.4.
44. *Quran*, 17/84.
45. Ibid., 2/269.
46. Ibid., 8/4.
47. Ibid., 10/62-64.

EPILOGUE

We may now conceive the relation of Islam to history as that of unity; not certainly of the abstract sort defying an objective explanation but synthetic in nature. Since faith in the unseen (*ghaib*) presupposes the growth of spiritual consciousness as against direct relationship of historical consciousness with everyday affairs, our concept of synthetic unity therefore implies both the difference and the unity of the depths rather than merely terms.

Muhammad did not found a new religion. Nor did he make a clean sweep of history by claiming absolute truth for a particular religion alone as compared with the distorted forms of the truth existing in the early seventh century religious cosmogony of West Asia. The spiritual consciousness experienced by him, though not independent of time, place, context and environment, had transcendent sanction for social action. But the very fact that social action itself was influenced by the Quranic concept of right (*ma'ruf*) and wrong (*munkar*) over a period of 22 years raises the last Prophet of mankind high above the historically-conditioned creative personalities. Spiritual consciousness is thus intrinsically a unity emanating from the felt-experience of being united with Allah and sending ripples to the darkness pervading the world, through inner stability of the soul and mind.

The concept of Divine Oneness (*Tawhid*) is, however, exposed to certain grave dangers if pushed to extremes. If one merely emphasizes the transcendence of Allah, one is prone to lose oneself in a welter of meaningless abstractions; and if one stresses the unity of Allah and man in the simplistic formula of pantheistic philosophy, a frightful anarchy of thought is sure to absolve human action of moral responsibility. What distinguishes Muhammad's role in history is his ability to make the unity of the Creator and created comprehensive to mankind in the moral responsibility of his action in accordance with the Divine injunctions. The Islamic concept of Divine unity generates a kind of consciousness within the bounds of one's spiritual and earthly life in the direction of uniting human behaviour and thought with the Mind of the *Quran*. That such a concept is not romantic is shown by innumerable religious teachers, Sufi missionaries, scholars and thinkers of Islamic history who enriched our knowledge of ourselves through adherence to the *Sunna*. Their names would have disappeared under a veneer of bogus conformity had not adherence to the model been essentially laden with the meaning of exaltation of character. Wasn't the serene influence of the Prophet's role on their souls and minds a creative force in the transformation of their average personalities? The evolution of Muslim societies would be unimaginable if we divorce adherence *(taqlid)* in the individual lives of creative personalities of Islamic history from the cherished goal of resolving spiritual and social tensions and conflicts into harmony and balance. History bears witness to the fact that individuals and groups either celebrated their virtues, built on their strengths and accepted several interpretations of the moral law *(Shari'a)*, or in certain cases, encouraged a climate of suspicion, distaste and fear. Our spiritual and historical consciousness, which now approximates to commonsense in a very broad sense, demands that we rejoice in our unity in diversity.

Any effort to understand unity in diversity in both the spiritual and historical context must include:

1. submission to the Word of Allah in letter and spirit;
2. the role of the prophets primarily as individuals; and
3. the response of societies to the divine mission and the resultant historical process as a whole. In considering these major aspects the concept of unity in diversity is crucial to comprehending both the Oneness of Allah in spiritual, and the diversity of societies in historical terms. Religion *vis-a-vis* history becomes meaningful only when viewed from the spiritio-historical perspective. The role of religion is therefore not to be viewed from a trans-historical perspective; nor can one merely understand the role of history from the so-called historical standpoint. Both religion and history would lose their spiritual and scientific meaning if either of them is divested of its intrinsic relation to the other. Neither religion nor history can acquire an objective meaning and purpose if they are

presented respectively as wholly sacred or wholly profane. Does religion corrupt historical thinking? Or have the so-called secular movements in history corrupted religion? Our purpose in raising such questions is to broaden and deepen our own understanding of the dual and reciprocal function of religion and society in not only generating but also easing the inner conflicts and social tensions of the human soul and mind respectively.

Spiritual consciousness is the movement of man in the direction of becoming objectively spiritual and historical. The unity of man in the movement of his gradual transmutation is a movement of his natural make-up. Being created in the best of moulds,[1] man, both as a spiritual and historical being, moves in the direction of the unity that links if not unites all diversities. Without the basic postulate of unity in diversity, he cannot understand the essential variation of response that personal qualities and character traits fostered under particular conditions of environment. Spiritual consciousness must therefore be viewed as religion in its pristine spirit and simplicity, emphasising individual ethical responsibility as its essential ingredient. And one achieves this consciousness only when one addresses one's soul and mind towards an understanding of the unity of human origin. To reach the unity of man in the spiritual and historical movement of his metamorphoses, a genuine quest for seeking knowledge beyond the ephemeral appearances of the world or beyond the "biologico-psychological plane of consideration", characterises the nature of the creative individual. Spiritual consciousness is the concomitant of a way of life within the bounds of the *Quran* and the authentically broader historical and human framework of the *Sunna*. Such a concept of life seeks to raise man out of the limits of physical time to descend into the sphere of Infinity. Although the *Quran* addresses itself to Infiniteness throughout, the following verses are central to the birth of several thought-patterns in our consciousness. "He is the First, He is the Last; and is the Manifest and Hidden and He has the knowledge of all that exists".[2] This eternal concept of the Infinite about His own Infinity helps us to resolve the basic contradictions in our consciousness towards an understanding of our own spirit and the dangers to which it is exposed in disparate mental make-ups and varying manifestations of ideological systems in space-time. Seen in this perspective, the Infiniteness of the Creator ceases to be an abstract concept on realising the extreme finiteness of our perceptions and goals *vis-a-vis* societies. True, the history of any society, in a specific time and place, is different from those of others. But it requires sublime intellectual effort in the Quranic sense to understand that spiritual awareness of being united in His Infinity provides us the keys to everything which happened in societies. But then the strength of Islam lies not merely in the seemingly abstract idea of Infinity but also in its historical assertion in the article of faith fundamental to Islam: "There is no deity but Allah and verily Muhammad is His servant and messenger". Did not Muhammad's role and its abiding influence on individual consciousness not only solidify but also ensure the genuine spiritual and historical traditions of Islam? In fact no other movement in Islamic history better provides an answer to such a question of vital significance as Sufism does. And Shaikh Nuruddin Rishi Kashmiri echoes the sentiments of the disciplined human souls of Islam in the following verse:

> I owned the *kalima*
> 'There is no deity but Allah'
> And consumed myself in the fire that it generates;
> Realising the mirage of existential unity,
> I found the Eternal.
> So I transcended space.[3]

The real meaning of the article of faith *(kalima-i-shahada)* becomes clear when one realises in one's growing consciousness that there is absolutely no problem worthy of reflection if it does not relate itself to the space-time dimensions of the *Quran*. Emphasizing the importance of the sincere and thoughtful act of professing faith in His oneness for a meaningful and purposeful existence, Nuruddin remarks:

> The meaning of *kalima* is the source of all knowledge;
> The good actions spring from self-restraint (in accordance with its spirit);
> The source of void is known to Him alone;
> His Infiniteness knows no bounds.[4]

Muslim societies have been characterised by tensions and conflicts, attributable to the very character of Islamic civilisation, intrinsically religious in contrast to being Western. Although

Islamic civilisation roughly flourished until the seventeenth century despite the visible cracks in the structures of such empires as the Mughal, the Saffavid and the Ottoman, it was exposed to the tremendous challenge of the Industrial Revolution of the West in the next century. Industrialisation led to modernisation which later came to be equated with Westernisation because of its historical ramifications. The colonisation of Muslim societies was a sequel to industrial imperialism. But Muslim struggle against all forms of imperialism, particularly economic and political, was motivated by nationalist rather than merely religious considerations. True, "revivalist" or "reformist" movements in Muslim societies revitalised the *Tawhidic* consciousness to a certain degree, but reformers could not go beyond the limitations of looking at their societies *vis-a-vis* Islam or *vice versa* from a rationale grounded in political pathos in contradistinction to the eternal objectives of Islam.

Eternity is not a world beyond human reason or vision. In the context of the *Quran* it is the Infinite time that embraces all forms of time. Eternity looks more revealing a concept with mathematical precision than accumulated knowledge stored in libraries, archives, museums and computers when an eternal love to satisfy the craving for truth grows within. A believer passes into eternity, or travels into Infinite time, while living in physical time with his heart's and mind's eyes ever fixed on the lifetime abode of the Creator and the created *(akhira)* in contrast to the transitory life on this planet. While the multitude of people do not have time consciousness, in the context of the *Quran*, to feel the reality of Infinite time *versus* the twiddling and twinkling of physical time, a traveller *(salik)* in the His Infinity constantly endeavours to find eternity affirmed in the sublime interaction of his disciplined soul, mind and behaviour.

Being crucial for a believer, time is the most serious concern of his probationary life. That he always strives to use the transitory stage of his existence to its sublimest end, i.e., death, is borne out by the highest importance he attaches to the final hour of his corporeal existence in this world. In the context of the Quran death does not come to destroy the real world of believers but that of those whose sensory organs have seldom passed through the threshold of sublime consciousness about the appointed time for the return of each soul unto Him. This reality makes itself more intelligible in the average human inclination to "grativate down to the earth"[5] in contrast to the integrated spiritual and historical consciousness of a believer that transcends it.

Spiritual and historical consciousness therefore fosters the natural idea of obedience to God by an 'automatic volition'—except for man, who has all the time to conquer or inherit the world according to his desires. Being bound up integrally with the time that knows no bounds, spiritual and historical consciousness knows no periods, no cut-off points. Although undefinable, yet it is comprehensible to both the soul and mind for which it holds a hope that never fades. Since the soul of an individual believer passes into eternity on self-realisation, the meaning of his life is derived from his relation to the spiritual and historical process. Taking spiritual and social responsibilities seriously, he makes his creativity felt and therefore moulds the historical process. Spiritual consciousness, in the ultimate analysis of the depths of our soul and mind, radiates. And in the context of the *Quran* and modern science nothing can travel faster than light. Since the speed of light is the same at every event and in every direction, its ripples can spread out as a circle in our consciousness if we are able to wriggle ourselves out of the lowest stage of 'gravitating down to the earth'.

Fazl al-Rahman rightly points out that "man does not require much effort to be petty, self-seeking, submerged in his day-to-day life, and a slave of his desires, not because this is 'natural' to him—for his real nature is to be exalted—but because 'gravitating down to the earth' as we have quoted from the Quranic language, is much easier than ascending to the heights of purity".[6] And when man 'gravitates down to the earth' in the name of what we call situational religious ideologies, he creates barriers that prevent the light from spreading out. Paradoxically, the standard-bearers of the so-called religious ideology, masquerading as beacons of light, find themselves uprooted from the original environment of Infinity in the continued failure of their romantic goals born out of temporal situations. The result of this rupture is what may be described as blurred boundary conditions in historical consciousness. Aren't ideologies of religio-political, secular and the Communist kind products of disorderly and chaotic thinking during the so-called periods of historical crisis? Doesn't the obsession with this world merely satisfy the conditions that are necessary for the existence of a civilisation, no matter how material or avowedly religious in character? And when the history of a civilisation is merely understood from a perspective limited in space and time, the spiritual and moral, nay, historical meaning of individual life loses relevance. Not the least, when the individual life is constructed as an end in itself for accomplishing certain ideological goals, the meaning of unity in diversity in both spiritual and historical terms is destroyed. We, therefore, view the concept of the 'New World Order' in the contemporary situation nothing more than a Utopian comedy of the Western mind. The tragedy or irony of this comedy is that this appallingly dangerous situation is a legacy of the 'scientific', 'secular', 'liberal' and 'progressive' minds of the West.

The *Quran* does not explain historical events in terms of the boundary conditions of physical time and mind. Although a point in space-time, particularised by its time and place, an event in the Quranic context is something that is bound to happen. "For every announcement there is a term..."[7] Here the reference is to time that is bound up with both individual and social actions during a limited timespan in our temporal reckoning. But the question concerning the time duration of societies or nations assumes a deeper significance when the *Quran* relates it to His purpose behind the creation of the universe. "And We created not the heaven and the earth and all that is between them in vain."[8] Hence, what we call present is not present in the dictionary sense but an unending linkage process between the past and future. Man's action at a particular moment or in a given situation links him to the past and future in the all-pervasive totality of the timeless Time. History as such is to be viewed not merely in the totality of temporal events but in the totality of the relationship existing between the Creator and the created. Whether man is deeply or partly conscious of this delicate, though not complex, relationship, or he is absysmally ignorant of spiritio-historical unity, his actions are liable to produce results in accordance with the Divine Judgment. Where the *Quran* brings home to us divine predetermination of everything, including human actions, it has recourse to a reasoning not in conflict with common sense. But where the *Quran* addresses men of intellect *(u'lul al-bab)*, it speaks to us in allegories. The emerging point is not the theocentric concept of history propounded in the *Quran* but anthropocentric. Since man's experiences and actions are measured and judged by Allah as *Qadir*, he becomes the most potential factor in the divine pattern of infinite beginning and the end of the cosmos.

Thus, in contrast to events of history in the apparently specific space-time relationship, the ultimate end of the world at one point of physical time has no boundary like that of the origin of universe. Significantly, the *Quran* does not specify the time of the end of the world. "Men ask you of the Hour. Say: The knowledge of it is with Allah only. What can convey (the knowledge) unto thee? It may be that the Hour is nigh".[9] Such a consciousness therefore makes the temporal world, described in the *Quran* as fleeting time, indistinguishable from the Infinite time even in being its integral component. Since man's death in the physical sense resolves the apparent contradiction of his relativity *vis-a-vis* fleeting time, the absorption of his soul in timeless unicity therefore becomes comprehensible in what we term the spiritio-historical relativity characterising the very structure of the *Quran*. The fundamental Quranic idea with regard to the law governing the immortality of the illumined soul is uniform for all reflective observers, no matter whether spiritually alive or dead. The influence of such individuals upon history is not equal to an extension of the self in physical time. Their personalities extend the physiological duration because in their consciousness the misuse of time amounts to the abuse of Allah's purpose of creation. The *Tawhidic Weltanschuung*, unlike ideological mental constructs of every kind, assumes universal relevance because of its all-pervading and all-embracing eternal relativity *vis-a-vis* soul (religion) and matter (history). As the *Quran* emphasizes the importance of Infinite Time with reference to fleeting time: "I swear by the time, that man is a certain loser save those who have faith and perform righteous deeds and counsel one another to follow the truth and to be steadfast."[10]

Faithfulness, righteousness, truthfulness and steadfastness are essential traits that exalt man in the *Quran* to unimaginable limits in undefinable Time *(Dahr)*. "Has there not been over man a long period of Time, when he was a thing unremembered?"[11] The question basically relates to the general and perennial problem of human nature and human behaviour. This is why spiritual leaders always acquainted themselves, as profoundly and objectively as they could, with the variegated variables and constants in human thought, feeling and action. And this also explains the fact that Islam, in the Prophet Muhammad's *Sunna*, emerges as *din al-fitra* rather than as an ideological product of his mind.

An ideology which goes beyond the very broad natural principles for founding a worldwide religio-political society—in sharp contrast to an ideal society deriving sustenance from its moral or natural code *(Shari'a)*—is bound to be historically conditioned. It may create a consciousness among a people necessary for offsetting the psychological, political and cultural dislocation in their own environment. But such a consciousness is just part and parcel of the historical process rather than the solution of the problem which intrinsically relates to the loss of human identity as a spiritual force *(khalifa)* to harmonise both the individual and collective thinking and behaviour for the universal good of mankind. Thus *din al-fitra* does not demand the acceptance of a worldwide religio-political identity, or the "New World Order" as a goal of history. For history is not for a natural religion the self-manifestation of a beginning without God, and its end without repentance; rather history is only an index of a conscious unity in diversity. But the question that remains to be answered is whether believers the world over are attuned to nourishing the eternal concept of the Nourisher of Worlds *(Rabb)* towards common activities and aims that the complexities and mysteries of the universe afford them! Shouldn't the *Quran* guide us?

Notes and References

1. *The Quran*, 95/4.
2. Ibid.
3. Ishaq Khan, *Kashmir's Transition to Islam*, p. 117.
4. Ibid.
5. *The Quran*, 7/176
6. Fazl-ur-Rahman, *Themes of the Quran*, p.19.
7. *The Quran*, 6/67
8. Ibid., *38/27*
9. Ibid., 33/63.
10. Ibid., *103/1-3*
11. Ibid., 76/1.

GLOSSARY

abd	servant
adhan	announcement; the call or summons to public prayers proclaimed by the crier *(muazzin)*
ahkam al-Hakimin	Absolute Ruler. The term occurs in the *Quran* for Allah.
ahl-i kitab	"The people of the Book." The *Quran* uses the term for Jews and Christians. Some sects of the Shias include the Magi *(Majusi)* under this term.
ahzab	"Confederates." The title of the 33rd chapter of the *Quran,* which was written when Madina was besieged by a confedration of the Jewish tribes with the Arabs of Mecca.
akhira	eternal abode
al-Amin	"The Trustworthy"
al-Basir	The All Seeing One; one of the Attributes of Allah as mentioned in the *Quran.*
al-Hamd	"Praise." The first chapter of the *Quran* is called after its first word, *al-hamd.* It is also called *surah-i fatiha.*
alif	first letter of the Arabic alphabet; symbol of Allah; numerical value 1.
alim al-ghaib	Knower of the unknowable or secret. It frequently occurs in the *Quran,* and means that Allah alone knows all that is hidden and is beyond human understanding and knowledge.
al-Wuddud	an Attribute of Allah meaning all-embracing love.
amanah	trust
ammara	the soul that, according to the *Quran* (12/59), is inclined to evil; also called *nafs-i ammara.*

anfus	self
annas	mankind
aql	reason; intellect
asabiyyah	social cohesiveness or solidarity
asma	names or attributes. The Attributes of God are called *asma al-husna*, excellent names.
ayat	pl. of *ayah*, sign, index or evidence of God. The term is also used for each verse of the *Quran*.
ayat-al-kursi	"The verses of the Throne." Verse 256 of chapter II of the *Quran*
azadi	freedom; independence
bismillah	"In the Name of Allah." An expression frequently used at the beginning of any undertaking by the Muslims.
dar al-amal	the abode of actions. It is through good actions alone that one can hope to live in the blessed abode *(dar al-na'im)* and the home of eternity *(dar al-khuld)* after one's death.
daula	government; power
dawah	invitation
din al-fitra	the natural religion. "And turn yourself to the primordial religion as a *hanif*, true to the natural religion which God made innate to all human beings. This natural endowment is universal and immutable in God's creatures. It is the true and valuable religion; but most people do not know." (*Quran*, 30/30)
din-i anif	the religion of Abraham. The word occurs several times in the *Quran* to show the sincerity and steadfastness of Abraham in the primordial religion.
durud	recitation of benediction
faqr	self-imposed poverty
fiqh	jurisprudence
furqan	one of the names of the *Quran*, meaning 'a discrimination'.
ghaib	secret, unknown
guru	teacher, spiritual preceptor

hadi	guide. The term invariably occurs in the *Quran* with reference to Allah as the Universal Guide.
hadith	sayings of the Prophet Muhammad based on the authority of a chain of transmitters. The Prophet uttered his words of wisdom at a given situation. His sayings *(hadith)* form the basis of Muslim life. The most authentic sayings were compiled in six volumes in the second half of the 9th century; among them, those of Bukhari (d. 870) and Muslim (d. 875), called *Sahihain,* are of particular importance.
hijra	migration; Muhammad's flight from Mecca in A.D. 622 is known as *Hijra.*
hikma	wisdom; prudence; it may consist of practical knowledge or of intuition concerning the Divine essence and Names.
hizb Allah	the party of Allah
ibad	servants of Allah; pl. of *abd*
ihsan	doing everything as beautifully as possible; perfection in spiritual terms which consists in worshipping God "as if you were seeing Him, for if you do not see Him, He sees you."
ijtihad	"exertion"; reasoning and reinterpretation. "The logical deduction on a legal or theological question by a *mujtahid* or learned religious scholar, as distinguished from *ijma,* which is the collective opinion of a council of divines."
ilah	an object of worship or adoration, i.e., a god or deity. The term Allah has a profound connotation with the definite article *al,* i.e., *al-ilah,* the God.
ilm-i ladunni	inner guidance
imam	one who leads the ritual prayers at a mosque; among Shias the leader of the community who is the descendant of the Prophet's son-in-law, Ali, and his daughter Fatima.
iman	faith; the inward aspects of Islam

insan-i kamil	perfect man
intifada	resistance
jahilyya	the period before the advent of Muhammad as the Prophet in Arabia is designated as the age of ignorance *(jahilyya)* *vis-a-vis* religious truths.
jihad	'holy war' incumbent upon Muslims against the tyranny, oppression and ethnocentrism of the 'infidels' under a religious leader *(imam)*; in terms of the deeper meaning of the *Quran* and, also, in the context of the *Sunna, jihad* is the culmination of an incessant struggle against base instincts of human beings living in a society characterised by moral atrophy.
jihad-i akbar	the greater warfare, which is against *nafs-i ammara* or the soul inclined to evil.
jihad-i asghar	"the lesser warfare." Sufis described the warfare against the "infidels" as of secondary importance in relation to the continuous struggle against the snares of one's self.
jihad bin-nafs	continuous and sustained struggle against the snares of the self or the soul and its base instincts.
jihad-bil-Quran	See *jihad-i Akbar.* "Therefore listen not to the unbelievers, infidels but strive against them with the utmost strenuousness with the *(Quran)*." See *Quran* (25/52).
jihad-i kabira	See *jihad-i Akbar* and *jihad-bin-nafs*
kafirun	pl. of *kafir,* infidel
kalim	the converser with Allah. The title given to the Prophet Moses in the *Quran* is *Kalim al-Allah.*
kalima	word; the profession of faith in Islam
kalima-i shahada	"The word of testimony." The belief is expressed in these words: "I bear witness that there is no deity but God, and that Muhammad is His Messenger."
Khabir	The Aware; one of the Attributes of Allah.
khalifa	pl. *khulafa.* Anglicised, "caliph", a successor, vicegerent, or deputy. The term is used in the

Quran for Adam, as the vicegerent of the Almighty on this planet. "And when thy Lord said to the angels, 'I am about to place a vicegerent *(khalifa)* on the earth,' they said, 'Wilt Thou place therein one who will do evil therein and shed blood?' *Quran* (2/28). Again: "O Daud (David)! verily We have made thee a vicegerent; judge then between men with truth." Ibid., 38/25.

The title of *khalifa* was given to the immediate successor of Muhammad, Abu Bakr, who was vested with the authority to rule and guide the *umma* in conformity with the *Quran* and the *Sunna*. The office of the first *khalifa* and his three successors Umar, Uthman and Ali was not hereditary; since a certain principle of election was adopted by the *umma* in respect of the first four *khulafa*. That is why they are known as the rightly-guided successors of the Prophet *(Khulafa-i Rashidun)*.

The Sufis, as against the religio-political interpretation of the *khulafa* of the latter times, attempted to revive the concept of the *khalifa* on purely spiritual foundations. Although the Sufis designated some of their disciples as *khulafa* in their own lifetime, it was not the hereditary element but the piety of a disciple that was emphasized most. The *khalifa* in Sufism was required to carry on the mission of the Prophet Muhammad and all other prophets before him through peaceful efforts aimed at stabilising and harmonising this world in a spirit of invitation *(dawah)* and dialogue.

khandaq   ditch

khanqah   The humble structure in which a Sufi lived; spiritual training was given in the *khanqah* and usually a public kitchen and other facilities were attached to it.

khatam-i nubbuwat	finality of the Prophethood
khatib	one who delivers the sermon or oration *(khutba)* before the Friday prayer in a mosque. The sermon is generally given by the *imam* of the mosque, though it can also be delivered by a guest speaker.
khilafa	the office of the *khalifa*
khilafat-i Rashida	the office of the first four rightly-guided *khulafa*. See also *Khalifa*.
kufr	infidelity
ladunna	His presence
lailat al-qadar	"The Night of Power and Excellence." A night in the month of Ramadan, described in the *Quran* as the one which excels thousand months.
lam	letter of the Arabic alphabet; numerical value forty; a mystic symbol.
lawwama	the soul that, according to the *Quran* (65/2) is self-reproaching and seeks God's grace and pardon after repentance and tries to amend.
ma'rifa	knowledge; gnosis
milad al-Nabi	the birthday of the Prophet Muhammad
mim	letter of the Arabic alphabet, numerical value forty, symbol of Muhammad; a popular tradition makes God say: "*ana Ahmad bila mim,* 'I am Ahmad (honorific name of Muhammad) without a'm, meaning thereby *Ahad,* 'One'. In the Sufi literature allusions to this well-known tradition are actually made to emphasize the Creator's love for the most perfect of human beings, i.e., the Prophet. Hence, one who strictly adheres to the *Sunna* of Muhammad endears himself to God.
mi'raj	ascension
muazzin	one who calls for prayers at regular intervals in a mosque; see also *adhan*.
mudhaddithun	pl. of *muhaddith;* the narrators of *hadith* or acts and words of Muhammad; those well-versed in the traditions.

mufsidun	pl. of *mufsid;* a foul dealer; a pernicious person. "God knows the foul dealer (*mufsid*) from the fair dealer (*muslih*)". *Quran*, 12/219.
muhib	lover
muhkamat	unambiguous verses of the *Quran*
mujhhadat al-nafs	streous efforts to guard one's self against its own snares.
mujtahid	one who strives to attain to a high position of scholarship and learning. This is the highest title conferred upon religious scholars of excellence and eminence. Although the four revered teachers and *imams* of the Sunnis and their immediate disciples were recipients of this title, it has also been bestowed on several others.
muminun	believers; plural of *mumin*, believer
munafiq	hypocrite. pl. *munafiqun*
munajat	fervent prayer (often chanted)
muqarrabun	those near to Allah
mushrikun	heretics; sing. *mushrik*
mutashabihat	allegorical verses of the *Quran*
mutmainna	the soul that, according to the *Quran* (79/27), is at peace. A true believer's soul returns to its Lord in an exalted state, i.e., it is at peace.
muttaqin	the pious; pl. of *muttaqi*.
nafs	the lower self; the lower instinct
n'at	poetry in praise of the Prophet; the tradition of reciting *n'at* aloud in chorus still exists in the mosques and shrines of the Kashmir Valley.
qadir	all-powerful
qutb	pole; axis; in *tasawwuf*: 'the pole of spiritual hierarchy.' The pole of a period is also spoken of; this highest member of the hierarchy of Sufis is often unknown to even the most spiritual of men.
Rabb al-alamin	Nourisher of the Worlds
rahma	mercy, compassion, grace bestowed by Allah. The attribute of grace is frequently dwelt upon in the *Quran* (7/54; 10/58; 6/133).

rasul	messenger
ridha	acquiescence; satisfaction
sabr	fortitude
salat	prayer
salihun	upright; pl. of *salih*
shahada	testimony; confession of Islamic faith
shari'a	Islamic law
sha'ur	consciousness of a special category
shifa	balm
sibgath	natural colour
Sunna	the tradition of the Prophet, his manner of life according to which the faithful should act.
taffakur	contemplation
tagut	an idol mentioned in the *Quran*
taqlid	a term used for strict adherence to the Islamic law without enquiry or examination.
tasawwuf	Islamic spirituality or Sufism
tawhid	'to declare that God is One'; monotheism; consciousness of one's oneness with God in the *Shari'a*-structured relationship; in this oneness the seeker is profoundly conscious of his servantship (*'ubudiyyat'*).
tawakkul	trust
ubudiyyat	servantship. When God mentions the Prophet Muhammad, He refers to his 'servantship' and says: "He revealed to His servant that which He revealed. "*Quran* (53/10)
ulama	pl. of *alim;* scholar-jurists upon whom the interpretation of the *Shari'a* rests.
ulama-i dunniya	the worldly *ulama* who associated themselves with the government and complied with a ruler's wishes, even if the latter flouted the religious law; usually cultivated such habits of mind and heart through their association with kings and rich people as were inimical to the growth of higher spiritual and ethical values in Muslim society; also known as *ulama-i su.*

ulama-i Haqq	the *ulama* whose interest is mostly directed towards the Hereafter.
ulul al-bab	men of intellect
umm al-kitab	"The Mother of the Book"; title used in the *Quran* (3/5) for the *Quran* itself. In the *Quran* (13/39), the term has the context of the preserved tablet, on which were written the decrees of God and the fate of humankind.
ummatan wasatan	community or nation of Islam is described in the *Quran* (2/143) as the 'median among the peoples of mankind'. The term can be understood as a stabilising and harmonising spiritual and social force among the comity of nations rather than in any political or ideological sense. For contrary view, see Ismail Raji al-Faruqi, *Tawhid: Its Implications for Thought and Life,* Preface.
ummi	unlettered
wahdat al-shuhud	unity of experience; implying that Allah and His seeker are joined together but their individuality is preserved. In this unity the seeker is profoundly aware not only of his individuality, but more importantly, of His beloved's unique individuality.
wahdat al-wujud	unity of being; it is experienced by an inflamed soul who believes that "Everything is He". That is how Ibn 'Arabi's ideas on the mystical experience were summarised in later mystical poetry, particularly in Iran, Turkey and India. The term has generally been misunderstood and misinterpreted.
wilaya	spiritual territories
zindiq	heretic

BIBLIOGRAPHY

Sources

I. *The Quran* (text).

II. *Translations and Commentaries of the Quran.*

Ali, Allama Yusuf, *The Holy Quran*, revised edition, King Fahd
    Holy Quran Printing Complex, Medina, 1989.
Arberry, A.J., *The Koran Interpreted*, London, 1953; New York,
    1964.
Azad, Maulana Abul Kalam, *Tarjuman al-Quran*, Calcutta, 1931,
    Vol. I.
Maududi, Maulana Abul Ala, *Tafhim al-Quran*, Lahore ed.
Mahmud al-Hasan, *al-Quran al-Hakim* (Urdu trans.), commentary
    by Shabir Ahmad Uthmani, Shah Fahd Holy Quran Printing,
    Medina, 1989.
Pickthall, M.M., *The Meaning of the Glorious Koran*, New York:
    New American Library and Mentor Books, n.d.
Shafi, Mufti Muhammad, *Maarif al-Quran*, 8 vols., Indian ed.
    Deoband, U.P. n.d.

III. *Hadith Collections*

Al-Bukhari, Abdullah Muhammad, Abu *Muqaddima Tajrid al-*
    Bukhari, an abstract of 1044 *ahadis* in original Arabic with
    Urdu translation, Malik Muhammad Din and Sons, Lahore,
    1936.
Al-Tabrizi, Wali al-din al-Khatib, *Mishkat al-masabih*, trans. James
    Robson, 4 vols., Lahore, Pakistan: Shaikh Muhammad
    Ashraf, 1971-73.

IV. *Tasawwuf*

Al-Ghazali, Abu Hamid Muhammad, *Kimiya-i Saadat*, Urdu
    trans. under the title *Ikseer-i Hidayat*, 20th ed. Newal Kishore,
    Lucknow, 1976.

Huwiri, Ali, *al-Kashf al-Muhjub,* Eng. trans. R.A. Nicholson, reprint, 1982, New Delhi.

Rumi, Jalaluddin, *Selected Poems from the Divani Shamsi Tabriz,* edited and translated, R.A. Nicholson, Cambridge University Press, Cambridge, Paperback, 1977.

V. *Secondary Works*

Ahmad, Akbar S., *Discovering Islam: Making a Sense of History,* Vistaar, New Delhi, 1990.

————, *Postmodernism and Islam; Predicament and Promise,* Penguin, 1992.

Ahmad, Imtiaz, *Caste and Social Stratification among the Muslims,* (edited), Manohar, New Delhi, 1973.

————, *Kinship and Marriage among Muslims in India* (edited), Manohar, New Delhi.

Bloch, Marc, *Feudal Society* (Eng. trans), London, 1961.

Bulliet, Richard, *Conversion to Islam in the Medieval Period: An Essay in Quantitative History,* Cambridge Mass, Harvard University Press, 1979.

Cragg, Kenneth, "Minority Predicament", *Journal of Muslim Minority Affairs,* Vol. XII, No. 1, Jan. 1991.

Esposito, John L., *Islam, the Straight Path,* Oxford University Press, New York, 1988.

————, *The Islamic Threat: Myth or Reality,* Oxford University Press, New Delhi, 1993.

Faruqi, Ismail Raji, *Islamization of Knowledge,* International Institute of Islamic Thought, 2nd ed., Indian reprint, 1988.

————, *Tawhid: Its implications for Thought and Life,* International Institute of Islamic Thought, U.S.A., 1982.

Carrel, Alexis, *Man the Unknown,* Penguin, New York, 1948.

Gibbon, Edward, *The Rise and Fall of the Roman Empire.* John W. Lovell Co., New York, Undated.

Guillaume, A., *The Life of Muhammad* (Eng. trans.), Oxford University Press, London, 1955.

Hitti, Philip K., *History of the Arabs,* London, 1951.

Hujwiri, Sayyid Ali, *Kashaf al-Mahjub* (Eng. trans.), Nicholson, Reprint, New Delhi, 1982.

Iqbal, Mohammad, *The Reconstruction of Religious Thought in Islam,* Kitab Bhawan, New Delhi, 1981.

Khan, Mohammad Ishaq, *Kashmir's Transition to Islam: The Role of Muslim Rishis*, Manohar, New Delhi, 1994.

————, "The Importance of the dargah of Hazratbal in the Socio-religious and Political Life of Kashmiri Muslims", in *Muslim Shrines in India*, ed. Christian W. Troll, Oxford University Press, New Delhi, 1989.

Larrain, Jorge, *The Concept of Ideology*, first Indian ed., Bombay, 1980.

Maududi, Abul Ala, *Towards Understanding Islam*, trans. and ed. Khurshid Ahmad, Delhi, 1967.

Mannheim, Karl, *Ideology and Utopia*, L. Wirth and E. Shills (trans.), Routledge and Kegan Paul, 1972.

Mujib, Mohammad, *Indian Muslims*, Montreal, London, 1969.

Qureshi, Ishtiaq Husain, *The Muslim Community of Indo-Pak Subcontinent* (1610-1947), Indian ed., Delhi, 1985.

Rahman, Fazlur, *Major Themes of the Quran*, Minneapolis and Chicago, Bibliotheca Islamica, 1980.

————, *Islam*, 2nd ed. Chicago, 1979.

Said, Edward, *Orientalism*, London, 1978.

Schimmel, Annemarie, "Reflections on Popular Muslim Poetry", *Contribution to Asian Studies*, Vol. XVII, Leiden E.J. Brill, 1982.

Smith, Cantwell, *Islam in Modern History*, Princeton: University Press, 1957.

Toynbee, Arnold J., *A Study of History*, London, 1934-54, Vol. VII; also abridged edition by D.C. Somervell under the same title in 2 vols. Oxford University Press, 1995.

Troll, Christian W., *Muslim Shrines in India* (ed.), Oxford University Press, New Delhi, 1989.

INDEX

salat, 48, 64, 112, 137
salihun, 10
salik, 161
Satan, 114, 132
Sayyid Ahmad Khan, 97, 98, 99
Schimmel, Annemarie, 90
Seculiarism, 17, 35
Self-Realisation, 111-126
Sha'afi, Imam, 18
Shahada, 22
Shari'a, 18-20, 41, 81, 88, 122, 130, 136, 151-153, 158, 165
Sha'ur, 27, 45
shifa, 2
Sibgath, 124; *Ullah,* 125
Singh, Dr. Karan, 30
Siva, 8
Spain, 116
Spanish Muslim, 117
Spiritual Ethics, 66
Srinagar, 92
Socialism, 97
Soviet Union, 17, 35, 115
Straight Path, 10, 42, 109, 111, 131
Sufism, 91, 101, 102, 104, 116, 117, 160
Sunna, 2, 12, 19, 21-24, 26, 49, 51, 55, 69, 74, 76, 77, 81-83, 88, 89, 91, 94, 102, 113, 118, 121, 129, 144, 150, 152, 158, 159, 165
Supreme Reality, 7
Supreme Reason, 8
Sura, 5, 9, 119

tadabbur, 45
tafakku, 45
Tagut, 132
ta'la, 98
taqlid, 158
taqlidi ulama, 139
Tara Chand, 90
tasawwuf, 41
tauba, 152, 154
tawakkul, 2, 147
tawhid, 19, 27, 55, 137, 157
Tawhid - Shari'a, 49

Tawhidic Weltanschuung, 6, 22, 29, 78, 95, 118, 138, 154, 164
Time 46, 87, 89, 93, 122, 131, 133, 150, 157, 159-165
Time magazine, 145
Toynbee, Arnold, 118
totalitarianism, 133

ubudiyyat, 64
ulama, 7, 18, 139, 140, 141
ulama-i-duniyya, 81, 140
ulama-i-Haq, 117
ulama-i-su, 81, 140
Ulami-i-haqq, 140, 141
u'lul-al-bab, 1, 6, 130, 146, 164
Umar, 44, 76
umma, 1, 3, 4, 23, 64, 79, 88, 89, 100-103, 113, 118, 120, 137, 138
Ummah, 98, 100
Umm al-kitab, 144
Ummat-i-Muhammadiyya, 17
ummi, 59
United Nations, 35
United States, 11, 17, 35, 114
Urwal ul-Wuthka, 132
USSR, 11, 14
Uthman, 44, 76-78

"Verse of the Throne", 132
Vishnu, 8

Wahabi, 135
wahdat al-shuhud, 47
wahdat al-wiyud, 47
wali, 125
Washington, 11, 17, 35
wiliya, 81
World Wars, 35
Wudud, 148

Yazid, 88

Zaid, 74
Zainab, 74
Zakat, 137
Zia-ul-Haque, 90
Zoroastrianism, 90